"This inspiring story of Merrel, Beth, and Arlene Callaway brought to mind the apostle Paul's statement "For me to live is Christ, to die is gain" (Phil 1:21). Pouring their lives out to spread the good news to unreached people groups in hard places, they joyfully accepted hardships, challenges, separations, and disappointments for the glory of God. I was both deeply challenged and encouraged."

—DAVE BRUNER,
Missions Pastor, East Cooper Baptist Church, Mount Pleasant, South Carolina

"Mortal Yearning reminds the reader what it means to live and die for Jesus. . . . Read this book. It allows the reader to borrow the genealogy of faith exhibited by the Callaway family—until you can establish your own generational, global faith."

—NIK RIPKEN,
author of The Insanity of God

"Mortal Yearning is an inspiring story of devotion and passion for Christ. Weaving vivid narrative with fascinating back-history, Godbold traces the years of her family's missionary service with skill and empathy. . . . This is a book that cannot be closed and forgotten. It speaks to the heart and begs a response."

—KAREN O'DELL BULLOCK,
B. H. Carroll Theological Institute

Mortal Yearning

Mortal Yearning

Three Callaways on Mission with One Passion

Joy Callaway Godbold

RESOURCE *Publications* · Eugene, Oregon

Resource Publications
An Imprint of Wipf and Stock Publishers
199 W. 8th Ave., Suite 3
Eugene, OR 97401

www.wipfandstock.com

PAPERBACK ISBN: 978–1-6667–3605–2
HARDCOVER ISBN: 978–1-6667–9386–4
EBOOK ISBN: 978–1-6667–9387–1

JANUARY 31, 2022 3:34 PM

Scripture quotations in this publication are taken from *The Holy Bible, King James Version,* in the Public Domain.

To the myriad Muslim and Hindu flowers
who mortally yearn for the living water—Jesus

Contents

Maps | ix

Acknowledgements | xi

Introduction | xiii

Chapter 1   A World What? | 1

Chapter 2   Up, Down, and All Around | 3

Chapter 3   Undergraduate Happenings | 5

Chapter 4   On Trek | 10

Chapter 5   Northern Jersey | 17

Chapter 6   Tall Corn State | 21

Chapter 7   "L'Étoile du Nord" | 26

Chapter 8   To Eastern Baptist and Beyond! | 30

Chapter 9   God's Timing | 35

Chapter 10   "Over the Bounding Main" | 40

Chapter 11   Hills of Zion and Mountains of Lebanon | 44

Chapter 12   Salam/Shalom— Where There Is No Peace | 51

Chapter 13   Destruction | 56

Chapter 14   Bahrain | 62

Chapter 15   Whither Goest Thou? | 73

Chapter 16   Moonlight over the Mediterranean | 79

Chapter 17   Victory between the Himalayas
              and the Brahmaputra | 89

Chapter 18   The Hashemite Kingdom
              and the Heavenly Kingdom | 100

Chapter 19   "Whither Thou Goest" | 112

Chapter 20   Constraining Love | 122

Chapter 21   Fruit Basket Upset | 137

Chapter 22   Regions Beyond | 142

Chapter 23   Thin Ice | 151

Chapter 24   *Arabia Felix* | 155

Chapter 25   Torn between Two Loves | 162

Chapter 26   Land of the Setting of the Sun | 166

Chapter 27   The Circuit Riders | 171

Chapter 28   Lighting A Candle | 180

Chapter 29   On Mission—A New One! | 185

Chapter 30   Christ the Solid Rock | 190

              Epilogue | 197

              Bibliography | 199

Maps

1. United Kingdom and the Republic of Ireland 1939

2. The Levant 1946

3. Bahrain and the Arabian Peninsula 1946

4. India with Assam 1949

5. North Bank of Assam, India 1949

6. Morocco

7. Yemen Arab Republic (YAR) and People's Democratic Republic of Yemen (PDRY) 1970

Acknowledgements

An ocean of gratitude swells within my heart upon my remembrance of you:

My Sunday school class, Pastor Jimmy and wife Brenda, and my Mount Washington Baptist Church family for their prayers and encouragement,

The Global Research team of the International Mission Board, SBC, who went above and beyond to supply numerous maps and photos: Scott Peterson, Global Research Manager, Steve McCord, Manager of Analysis and Reporting, and Jim Courson, Senior GIS Analyst,

PC Solutions, Campbellsville, KY, with Drew Sin, Travis Perkins, and owners Kim and Steve Arnold, without whose technical help the manuscript would have shriveled on the vine,

All-in-Our-Family friend Rebekah Travis of Rebekah T. Photography, who worked magic with her lens,

The professionals at Wipf and Stock for guiding this vintner through the perplexing path to publication,

Callaway cousins, nieces and nephews, and other family members whose generosity allowed the fruit to ripen well,

Web Master Par Excellence Rhonda Dragomir, who from miry clay made something beautiful,

My oh-so-busy Endorsers, who took the time to read and evaluate *Mortal Yearning,*

Best Editor Ever Linda Harris, who pains-takingly did what editors ever do best,

Acknowledgements

My beloved sisters and brothers-in-love, who picked off the undesirable insects and mold that threatened to blight the product, patiently endured my litany of woes, and rendered invaluable advice,

My tech-savvy children Ty, Sean, Cliff, and Jesse and daughters-in-love LauraBeth, Jenni, and Lindsay, who unraveled tangled computer vines long- and short-distance, deposited months of work "in the cloud," and enheartened me in many ways. They are God's gracious gift to my husband and me.

My older grandsons, Samuel and Owen, who thought having an author in the family "is cool." (The younger ones really didn't care.) They are all icing on the fruitcake.

My husband, Lewis Blakeley, for his cheerful sacrifice of time, attention, meals, and money and for his unfailing support and love throughout this process,

And my Heavenly Father, who sustained during the journey.

Thank you all!

Joy Callaway Godbold

Introduction

Why the title *Mortal Yearning*? Sidney Lanier's poem "Song of the Chattahoochee" tells the tale of a real river. It begins its journey in northeastern Georgia—in Lanier's day in the counties of Habersham and Hall. The river rushes downward, ignoring the enticements of actual gemstones embedded in Georgia soil, of trees, grasses, and boulders that seek to slow or block its path. The river's passion is to feed the thirsty flowers below; they will die without its life-giving water.

A high school English class introduced Lanier's poem to me. I saw it as a metaphor of the consecrated Christian life. Christ commanded us: "Go, . . . baptize, . . . teach, . . .; ye shall be witnesses unto me" (Matthew 28:19–20; Acts 1:8).

The final stanza of Lanier's poem speaks of "a myriad flowers" that "mortally yearn" for the river's water. A myriad, a countless number of people across our globe, long for, yearn to hear of a God who loves them. Tragically, they are spiritually dying without Christ, the Water of Life.

Song of the Chattahoochee

Sidney Lanier (1842–1881)

Out of the hills of Habersham,
Down the valleys of Hall,
I hurry amain to reach the plain,
Run the rapid and leap the fall,
Split at the rock and together again,
Accept my bed, or narrow or wide,
And flee from folly on every side
With a lover's pain to attain the plain

Far from the hills of Habersham,
Far from the valleys of Hall.

All down the hills of Habersham,
All through the valleys of Hall,
The rushes cried "Abide, abide,"
The willful waterweeds held me thrall,
The laving laurel turned my tide,
The ferns and the fondling grass said "Stay,"
The dewberry dipped for to work delay,
And the little reeds sighed "Abide, abide,
Here in the hills of Habersham,
Here in the valleys of Hall."

High o'er the hills of Habersham,
Veiling the valleys of Hall,
The hickory told me manifold
Fair tales of shade, the poplar tall
Wrought me her shadowy self to hold,
The chestnut, the oak, the walnut, the pine,
Overleaning, with flickering meaning and sign,
Said, "Pass not, so cold, these manifold
Deep shades of the hills of Habersham,
These glades in the valleys of Hall."

And oft in the hills of Habersham,
And oft in the valleys of Hall,
The white quartz shone, and the smooth brook-stone
Did bar me of passage with friendly brawl,
And many a luminous jewel lone
—Crystals clear or a-cloud with mist,
Ruby, garnet and amethyst—
Made lures with the lights of streaming stone
In the clefts of the hills of Habersham,
In the beds of the valleys of Hall.

But oh, not the hills of Habersham,
And oh, not the valleys of Hall

Avail: I am fain for to water the plain.
Downward the voices of Duty call—
Downward, to toil and be mixed with the main,
The dry fields burn, and the mills are to turn,
And a myriad flowers mortally yearn,
And the lordly main from beyond the plain
  Calls o'er the hills of Habersham,
  Calls through the valleys of Hall.[1]

---

1. Lanier, "Song of the Chattahoochee," *Poems of Sidney Lanier*, 24—25. In the public domain.

CHAPTER 1

A World What?

1933

A huge poster touted, "*Chicago World's Fair 1833—1933 A Century of Progress!*" The exhibition promised displays of the latest technology, the brightest new ideas, incredible inventions, and astounding futuristic plans.

Merrel Callaway had dreamed of going. What a fantastic adventure! Known to his seven older siblings as Meck, he never expected to visit Chicago. As much as his parents loved him, on a pastor's salary they could not send him round trip from Jacksonville, Florida, to Chicago.

Then an intriguing word whispered through his high school. The Florida All-State Boys' Band would perform at the fair. Meck investigated what instruments the band still needed. Powered by gritty determination and his Callaway musical genes, Meck learned to toot the trumpet in short order. His work paid off.

He climbed on the bus with the other Florida All-State Band boys. The rollicking trip northward included stops to entertain folks in cities along their route.

The exhibition in Chicago offered more than Meck had imagined. Booths dotted the landscape, promoting specialty foods, health, religions and denominations, and Bible translation. Companies advertised their latest exciting new products—portable typewriters, vacuum-packed coffee, and cleaning products. Fairgoers learned uses of chemicals, metals, and gemstones, and the making of paper. Balloon and air races thrilled the crowds.

Meck examined a proposed highway system. The intricate model revealed tight cloverleaf curves twisting on and off speedways. Could that actually be built? *Probably not*, he mused.

The Florida band entertained the throng of onlookers with rousing musical selections. Their schedule permitted one free afternoon for exploring the Windy City.

Meck looked forward to visiting Moody Bible Institute. His father, Timothy Walton Callaway, also known as T.W., had spent a year studying at Moody before Meck's birth. Meck hoped to see the gigantic auditorium he had heard so much about.

He located the school. To get in, he had to pass big signs advertising speakers and conferences. He explored the auditorium. As he came out and was looking at a large poster, who should be looking at the next one but Brother Davidson, a great family friend! Meck hadn't expected to run into him in Chicago, of all places.

Davidson, a godly Scotsman, spoke in churches about his missionary work in China when on furlough. He stayed with the Callaways from time to time, in Meck's sister Rosa's room, since she enjoyed the best furniture and had the most comfortable room.

If Brother Davidson failed to spot oatmeal on the breakfast table, he would poke young Meck and whisper, "Tell your mother she forgot the porridge."

One morning, the gentleman came downstairs lamenting, "I've lost my teeth!"

A teeth hunt ensued. In her search, Rosa went into her room and picked up Brother Davidson's pillow. She screamed, "His teeth nearly bit me!"

Meck and the missionary met moons later by the Moody posters. Mr. Davidson confided in his Scottish brogue, "Merrel, ever since you were a little boy at Park Place in Macon, then Chattanooga and Jacksonville, I've been praying that God would give you a world vision."

A world vision? He wondered what Brother Davidson had come up with now. Meck thought he was a funny old man who didn't know what he was talking about!

CHAPTER 2

Up, Down, and All Around

1916

As Brother Davidson implied, bouncing from state to state dotted Meck's childhood. Born in Dublin, Georgia, in 1916, Meck remembered the parsonage at his father's church in Macon. "To get to Sunday school from our house, you had to go downhill. I remember rolling down the grassy bank toward the street below in my nice white-and-navy sailor suit."

His father commented, "Merrel was unusually active in mind and body. When my youngest was a small boy, an uncle offered him a nickel every time he could run through a rolling tire. That day his piggy bank was replenished with several nickels."

When he was four or five, Meck's family uprooted to Chattanooga, Tennessee, where his father had accepted another pastorate. After a communion service, a prominent lady who worked for the church emerged from the study to find Meck guzzling the grape juice from the leftover tiny cups.

Meck made friends with young Hopie Davies from a Presbyterian family. One day, the two lads played church. Meck preached and Hopie led the singing. "I was showing Hopie how my father baptized people. Down by the barn were all these little bitties or baby chicks Papa had bought. To my amazement, after I'd baptized them in the name of the Father, Son, and Holy Spirit, three or four of them started walking around, then fell over dead! Papa took me back down to the same barn and threatened me with a spanking. He reminded me, 'Thou shalt not kill.'"

Another day, he asked his father for a nickel. "Not today, Merrel, but tomorrow."

Quickly came the answer, "Give it to me today, Papa; there ain't no tomorrow. When tomorrow comes, it's but today."

His papa admitted, "The little philosopher got the nickel."

When a lad of six, his chore was closing the chickens in the coop every evening. Once he forgot. His mother fussed, "Merrel, I will have to do your job. It is dark and I'm afraid to go to the chicken yard."

Meck quoted Psalm 56:3 to her. "Why, Mama, you ought to be ashamed! 'What time I am afraid, I put my trust in the Lord,'" he wisecracked.

When he was in seventh grade, his family relocated to Cleveland, Ohio. There he earned money delivering newspapers on his bike. When he joined the Pocket Testament League, he carried a thick New Testament in his hip pocket. Consequently, it was tearing down the pocket.

Mother Callaway spoke to Meck about this.

"But I could not go to school without it," he argued, "for when I get in a fight, I just pull out the Sword of the Spirit and pop the other fellow with it!"

T.W.'s pastorates moved the family to Waycross, Georgia, then Jacksonville, Florida. Though Meck broke his nose playing football at Robert E. Lee High School, he hid this from his long-suffering mother.

So far, Meck's "world vision" encompassed a few southern states and Ohio. Were Brother Davidson's prayers useless?

CHAPTER 3

Undergraduate Happenings

1933

A FTER high school, Meck received a dubious offer he didn't want to refuse. In that era at the theater between movies, comedians presented
minstrel shows, cracking jokes and singing silly songs. Meck was intrigued
and asked his father's advice. "Look, Papa, I would travel all over the country; I'd travel all over!"

Meck admitted, "Papa did right by very tactfully saying, 'If you just
stay in God's will, you'll do more traveling than you ever dreamed of.'"

Years later, Meck added, "Thank the Lord, I listened to Papa and instead went to Norman Park Junior College near Moultrie and Summerville,
Georgia."

There Meck again played football. "We were the southern college and
Truett-McConnell the northern college—football rivals. In a pep rally before a game, the coach of Truett-McConnell was asked to say a few words.
He said, 'We're so glad to be down here to our sister college, because she's
the weaker vessel!'"

Meck described another game:

> I was the safety man on the team. I was so small they couldn't trust
> me any closer. The second time I broke my nose was when we were
> up against a full-year college. I rode with the coach to the game.
> He told me about a young quarterback at Mercer College who was
> also small. This quarterback had a way when, even in a head-on
> tackle, he'd ride up in the air in a little ball. Then he'd just unload
> right into [his opponent's] midsection . . . knocking him down like
> an explosive bomb.

So, during my game, I saw this big fullback coming toward me. Everybody else was back there and the goal was here. All I could think of was, "Don't forget the bomb!"

He was expecting me to wait on him. I ran as fast as I could toward him. He was running fast too, so we met earlier than he expected. I bounced off him. For the second time in my football career, I landed on my nose. I heard the crowd roaring, just going wild, and I was sure he had made a touchdown. But when I looked around, he was on the ground. All I did was trip him up. Afterwards, a coach I'd had before said, "Way to go, Callaway!" It made me feel so good!

The Christmas holidays came and went. Meck returned to Norman Park:

When I went back the second semester, I found that my roommate had been kicked out. They had taken out his top bunk and he had taken all his pictures off the walls. It was more like a prison cell.

I got convicted about some of the things I had done the first semester. Consequently, I doubted my salvation. I had thought that I was saved when I was seven years old and was baptized. But if I'd been saved, why was I living like this—football, popularity, and all that?

Then I remembered something in the gospel of John. I had to take my Bible out of the trunk where Mama had packed it. I laid it on the bed and started reading. I read John 1:11–13: "He came unto his own and his own received him not. But as many as received him, to them gave he power to become the sons of God, even to them that believe on his name: which were born, not of blood, nor of the will of the flesh, nor of the will of man but of God."

I just looked at that for about ten minutes. I said, "Lord, I'm not sure what receive means; but I'm sorry for my sins; and whatever receive means, I do that right now." I may have been ten or fifteen minutes on my knees. I told him, "I received you, I must have received you, I did receive you; therefore, I must be a child of God. I must be saved." I don't think I've doubted my salvation since then. That's when I got the assurance of my salvation.

Within a month, a group of us guys decided to have a dormitory prayer meeting one night a week. I was the first one to speak. I remembered Papa's sermon, "Woe, Lo, and Go," from the sixth chapter of Isaiah: "Woe is me! for I am undone. I am a man of unclean lips . . . Lo" [verses 5, 7]; this is live coals from the altar touching [my mouth] and purifying me, saving me, cleansing me. "Whom shall I send and who will go for us?" [verse 8]. So, I preached to those guys.

In the first semester, someone had heard that I played the trumpet with the Florida All-State Boys' Band. Later, in the high school band, I had also played the mellophone. (It had a big mouthpiece, bigger than a French horn, which you played with the fingers of the other hand.) At college, they said, "If you can play a mellophone, you can play a harpoon [harmonica]." So, we played at a couple of dances and were paid maybe a dollar apiece.

One of the boys' father was a chiropractor who knew of a chiropractic school out in Kansas. My friend suggested that the two of us travel there, form a little band to make money, and enroll in the chiropractic college. So, I wrote Papa, "What would you think of me being a chiropractor?" We had a relative in Macon who was married to a chiropractor. Papa wrote Dr. Jones. The doctor wrote me a letter, telling me all about what a chiropractor does. I was serious enough about the idea.

But the more I prayed about it as a Christian, God said, "No, I want you to be a preacher." I wrote Papa back and said, "I believe God wants me to be a preacher."

Meck then remembered one of his football coaches:

When this man graduated from Mercer, he was called to preach. But he'd also had some education courses. That way he could make money by teaching school, even if he took a half-time job at a church that didn't pay much. I wrote Papa, "Could I take a course in education and do this: Be a preacher, but have this to fall back on?"

Papa wrote back, "I didn't advise you on the chiropractic thing, but I believe I'm in a position to give you some advice on this. What I would suggest is, if God has called you to preach, set your education to be a preacher—study to be a preacher!"

His sophomore year, Meck transferred to the University of Chattanooga and lived at home. His father told him about the Chattanooga Bible Institute. Not really a college, it nonetheless provided some of the country's best Bible teachers. Workers could listen to them on their lunch hour. Meck had morning classes. Within five minutes, he arrived at these lectures.

Years earlier, Meck's father and Dr. Bob Jones had preached together on the streets of Macon. "Papa said that at that time Bob Jones had the sweetest spirit." Jones had started a college named after himself in Cleveland, Tennessee. When he heard that his friend T.W. had a son attending the University of Chattanooga, he insisted, "Tell Walton Callaway to get that boy over here!"

Dr. Jones promised Meck a scholarship. He explained, "Papa couldn't refuse this; it was so cheap. I went there my junior and senior years."

Just like his older brother Timothy or "T" at Mercer University, the student body elected Meck president. After the vote, a girl called him into a room with a piano. She made it clear that, since they both held student body offices, they could get away with kissing on the sly. Blind eyes, according to her, would be turned to their infraction. Meck declined.

Perhaps because T.W. had been raised in Americus, Georgia, the paper there announced Merrel Callaway's college completion. "When Papa's cousin Merrel Price Callaway, a New York banker, saw my name in his hometown Americus newspaper, he called Papa. He asked why they had not named me Merrel Price Callaway. He said it was the Price family that connected us to George Washington. From then on, I became Merrel Price Callaway." Much later, he would quip that his middle name was adopted, "because every Callaway has his 'price.'"

Cousin Merrel offered to pay Meck's fees to any school he wished to attend. His cousin also invited him to live with his family in New York City and attend Columbia University. Meck accepted the last two offers.

The older Merrel wanted his namesake to go into banking with him or into law, but the scholar continued on his path toward ministry. Because Bob Jones College was not then accredited, Columbia refused its credits. The new graduate repeated his junior and senior years. Among other classes, he enrolled in Classical Greek. Regarding subjects, Meck explained, "I tried to spread myself as far as I could, 'cause I considered three years of seminary my major."

Life in the Big Apple proved exciting. At a café one day, a man plopped down at his table and asked, "Would you like to play a game of cards?"

Meck had never learned, so said, "No, thanks." Later, he discovered that the fellow was a gambler who fleeced green young men, pocketing their money. Hence, years afterward, Meck never allowed cardplaying in his home.

Cousin Merrel purchased season opera tickets each year. Meck jumped at the chance to attend, often with his cousin's daughter, Mary. But he recounted that his life included more than studies and entertainment:

> I helped out at the Bowery Mission and preached on the streets with
> the League of Evangelical Students, which predated InterVarsity

Christian Fellowship. My Georgia accent and revival-style preaching drew the crowd. Then the intellectuals would take over and speak to the university students. The *Columbia Daily Spectator*, the university's weekly newspaper, joked in bold print about these young preachers bringing revival to the campus.

Meck spent the summer of 1939 in the British Isles. He hoped to attend the International Conference of Evangelical Students as a delegate and the famous Keswick Conference. He never forgot those four months he spent giving and getting blessings. But he could not have imagined what was in store for him there. The Third Reich was on the move.

CHAPTER 4

On Trek

1939

G ERMANS had torpedoed the *Lusitania* off the coast of Ireland during World War I. Merrel sailed with a round-trip ticket on the *Samaria*, a sister ship owned also by the Cunard Line. To his parents Merrel penned, "We had a wonderful crossing, although we were in fog twice and saw two icebergs. I felt a little nauseated at breakfast one morning, when nearly everyone else skipped a meal; but I went ahead and ate prunes and liver. About fifteen minutes later, I made a grand dash for the rail, but did not quite make it. Luckily, no one was on deck but myself."

As Merrel's ship docked at Liverpool, a uniformed courier asked for a Mr. Callaway. The courier brought a message from a Reverend Drysdale of Emmanuel Bible School in Birkenhead. This principal invited him to spend a couple of days there. Merrel later suspected that Brother Davidson of "world vision" fame had orchestrated this encounter.

Merrel met with Brother Drysdale in his office. He asked Merrel what his plans were for the summer. He told Drysdale about the International Conference of Evangelical Students held at Cambridge. The principal responded, "Tiny Palmer is a member and graduated from Cambridge himself. Let me get you in touch with him."

Drysdale arranged a meeting with Tiny Palmer, a vicar of the Church of England. "Tiny" was at least seven feet tall. "Before we separated," Merrel wrote, "I had had low tea, high tea, three cards of introduction, and a letter of introduction to one of the chairmen of the Cambridge conference. I also enjoyed a prayer meeting with him in his study and a promise to meet again at Keswick."

Map of the United Kingdom and the Republic of Ireland, 1939
(Map courtesy of Steve McCord, Manager of Analysis and Reporting, and Jim Courson,
Senior GIS Analyst, International Mission Board, SBC)

Merrel described his trip to Cambridge:

I passed seven or eight army airdromes. In one of them, there were 7,000 balloons, which may be blown up and used as a barrage around London. Enemy airplanes would run into the wires holding them and would have their propellers knocked off. Another was an underground airport. The planes were lowered on elevators (or "lifts," as they call them) and concealed from the enemy. In Birkenhead Navy Yard, I saw one of the nine-ninety-ton destroyers being built.

The Liverpool Cathedral had the handle to a door in the "Lady Chapel" made in the forms of a lizard and a snail. Thus, not forgetting that God not only created and watches over the great things, but also the mall and unimportant things to his everlasting glory—small and unimportant things such as I.

The conference was the best thing in Cambridge. There were 750 students from thirty nations all exalting the blood of Christ. Sunday night, . . . the head of the Keswick Conference made a missionary plea which challenged us all. As yet, I still don't know that God wants me on the foreign fields. If he does, he has two or three years to make it clear to me.

Before the conference was over, Merrel had invitations to speak at three boys' camps—one in the stunning Lake District of Kent and two in the Channel Isles of Wight and Guernsey.

In letters to his family, Merrel catalogued his adventures around England before and between acting as camp chaplain:

Yesterday, I visited the church of St. Mary Woolnoth on Lombard Street across from the Bank of England. John Newton preached there for forty years. It is also the church of William Wilberforce. An epitaph reads, "John Newton, Clerk, once an infidel and libertine, a servant of slaves in Africa, was by the rich mercy of Savior Jesus Christ preserved, restored, pardoned, and appointed to preach the faith he had long labored to destroy."

In Westminster Abbey, around the plaque of Jenny Lind, are the words, "I know that my Redeemer liveth." Below the tablet to John and Charles Wesley is "I look upon all the world as my parish," and "God buries his workmen, but carries on his work." I enjoyed Bunhill Cemetery, where Isaac Watts, John Bunyan, Daniel Defoe, John Owen, and Susannah Wesley are buried. John Wesley is buried in the chapel opposite. I made a point to find Susannah's grave, which is unpretentiously over in an obscure corner; while her son's is so prominent. I'd rather have seen hers than his, because she deserves most of his glory.

I've been lucky to see the House of Commons in debate. The other day when I was looking through the fence at Buckingham Palace, the young Queen was talking to two men in a front room. An old Irish woman next to me waved to the Queen and—John Brown!—if the Queen didn't wave back!

I went on a "tram" or street car to Greenwich, where the Prime Meridian is or where it starts from. I spat squarely right in the middle of the Prime Meridian for causing me so much trouble in Astronomy.

Two members of the Royal Navy College there took me all over the college. The boys told me that the night before, when the King was there, quite a few had imbibed pretty heavily by the time dinner was over. Some of the boys were playing leapfrog in the lounge. To the amazement of all, two Admirals and one cabinet member began also playing leap frog, jumping over one another staggeringly well. His Majesty walked into the lounge and said, "As you were," which either made them relax—or not.

Last Sunday, I preached at Tadworth Free Church and that night at Billingsgate Mission, a mission for those who live around the famous Billingsgate Fish Market—famous for fish and fish smells.

At the London Tower, where the Crown Jewels are kept (and were they unbelievable!) and where Ann Boleyn, Lady Jane Grey, and others, including Walter Raleigh, were put to death, I met two American girls. One of them said that a German soldier had warned them to be out of Germany by August fifteenth, when the harvest season is finished. However, I'm sure he was wrong! I absolutely agree with the US publishers of *Life*, when they said that there would be no war for at least a year.

I am now in Keswick after a bus ride on which we passed near Nottingham, Sherwood Forest (saw about fifty baby deer). We passed through Nottingham during England's largest "blackout" to date. All car lights are dimmed; all other lights out so that airplanes could not see where to drop bombs. However, don't worry about a war. England and Germany are so well prepared that they're afraid to start now. Hitler missed his chance at Munich.

I visited St. Clements of Old Romney Church, built in or before AD 791 in Saxon times. There's a "leper's squint" or hole in one of the inside walls which lepers could look from the outside into the altar while people were in church. In Saxon times, the congregation sat on the floor.

In Kent, Merrel served as chaplain to about seventy youngsters from the Home for Little Boys and enjoyed it immensely. "So far, most of their questions have regarded American cowboys and gangsters. Boys are boys anywhere, it seems! The camp was used mightily of the Lord in soul-winning and deeper spirituality. The boys themselves had prayed for their friends' salvation."

At the camp on the Isle of Wight, Merrel shocked the lads by coming out to speak in his tennis shorts, which rode up higher than their Bermudas.

Merrel thought Guernsey the most beautiful of the Channel Islands. From there he could view France, with Jersey nearby. Cattle are not imported on the two isles, he learned, for fear of corrupting the famous Guernsey and Jersey breeds.

Merrel summed up his three camp experiences. "That all helped give me Brother Davidson's 'world vision.'"

Merrel's cousin Mary, now at Vassar College, had failed to buy a British racing bicycle as a "badge" of having toured Europe. Cousin Merrel sent him funds to buy one for his daughter. An elder or deacon at a church at which Merrel had spoken that Sunday owned a hardware store. He agreed to sell the racer at a reduced price. Merrel wanted to visit Ireland by way of North Wales. The owner offered to drive him to the Welsh border. Up before dawn Monday morning, they chose a bike from the store and loaded it into the back of the car. At the creek that divides England from Wales, a soldier stood at attention, guarding the bridge with his rifle. The two in the car expressed shock and puzzlement.

"Where have you been? Don't you know there's a war on?" the soldier admonished.

The driver didn't believe in listening to the wireless on Sundays, so he and Merrel hadn't heard that England and France were at war with Nazi Germany.

Merrel caught the ferry over to Ireland. Early in the morning rain, a policeman stopped him and looked down at Merrel's shorts. "Why don't you put on some clothes when you come out in public?" About a foot stretched between the American's knees and his tennis shorts. The officer let him go.

Merrel notified his parents that he might be late to seminary, as he had agreed to a ten-day evangelistic campaign in Bath, England.

When word spread that France and England had declared war on Germany, Merrel's boat ticket on the *Samaria* went to a child or woman evacuating to America. He found passage on a freighter in early October bound for Philadelphia.

The editor of his hometown paper requested that he write of his time in England. Excerpts read:

> England in wartime is a land of contrasts. At the once stately old Canterbury Cathedral, I was greeted by the sight of plain glass windows instead of the priceless stained glass once there. The National Art Gallery and the British Museum . . . the famous Tussaud's Wax Museum . . . [are] now boarded up in front. It was interesting to contrast the sandbag-supported windows [of Buckingham Palace] from which a month earlier I saw the Queen wave to an old Irish woman.
>
> The greatest inconveniences to the tourists during wartime are the wrecking of train schedules and the blackouts. Dr. Donald

Grey Barnhouse, who held a Bible conference and evangelistic campaign in Chattanooga, was holding a similar campaign in Belfast when I was in Dublin, Ireland. Because of the blackout, he was compelled to preach to 3,000 people in total darkness. There are other inconveniences, such as being pulled out of bed at two a.m. by an air raid siren, which sounds like the amplified wail of a gigantic dying cat . . .

While waiting for my boat to sail from Avonmouth, I watched two 15,000-ton steamers, loaded with guns, ambulances, and soldiers, sail away. We waved to them what may have been the last familiar "cheerio" that those unfortunate Tommies will ever hear again.

I was disgruntled with the American Consul when he suggested that I exchange my Cunard Line ticket for a crossing on a freighter. I was even more fearful when I saw the empty barrels on the top deck in which aviation Ethyl fluid had been brought from Boston to England after the war had begun. Also, the freighter pitched so badly in the rough Northern Atlantic that the Captain and several members of the crew fell out of their bunks one night, while the passengers held tight and prayed. However, my dissatisfaction with the freighter was overcome today when I read that the other boat upon which I desired passage—the *President Harding*—had run into a storm at the same position, with one person killed and scores injured.[1]

The cargo ship had, in fact, illegally carried aviation fluid to Allies before the USA had entered the war. As Merrel said, "This aviation fluid could only be for airplanes to bomb the Nazis. So, if a Nazi pilot looked down and saw all those cans, he'd bomb the daylights out of us!"

But the freighter wallowed safely across the Atlantic to Pennsylvania.

Merrel's three years at Eastern Baptist Seminary would melt the strident edges of his spiritual heart. He identified this change:

Aside from my freshman year at Norman Junior College [a Baptist school], where God called me to the gospel ministry, I had attended religiously independent and secular colleges and universities. I had become a religious independent at heart and quite pharisaic in my smugness.

(But God) detained me in holiday in England, at the outbreak of World War II, forcing me to enroll in Eastern Baptist Seminary. It began late on its new campus. It was there that I began to

1. Merrel P. Callaway, "Callaway Recites Thrilling Escape," *Chattanooga Free Press,* October 21, 1939.

understand the valid arguments for "lighting a candle, instead of cursing the darkness"[2] in other New Testament churches. I am thankful for the loving spirit that I observed there.

But at Eastern, Merrel's heart would be pierced by two arrows.

---

2. Variation on a quotation first attributed to William L. Watkinson in 1907. In the public domain.

CHAPTER 5

Northern Jersey

1921

E LIZABETH Prior Fountain, born May 1921, blossomed into adulthood in a comfortable, upper-middle class home in Chatham Township, New Jersey. Her father, Guion, adored her, her mother, Florence (or Flossie), loved her, and two younger sisters Joyce and Audrey, well, they were sisters. Relatives from nearby Plainfield visited many Sunday afternoons and holidays.

Guion wrote missives to all his young daughters. To two-year-old Elizabeth (Beth or Betsey), he penned, "You are still a very lovely baby—a perfect beauty. People look at you everywhere you go and talk about you. Person after person says you are the prettiest girl they have ever seen and they mean it when they say it. And you are a good tot!"

Fountain men attended Yale University, not other Ivy League schools. Guion recounts, "When Beth was seven years old, she, her mother, and others went to a ball game at Princeton. When Beth got home, she said, 'Well, the grounds at Princeton are beautiful and the buildings are wonderful. It must just be the college itself is no good!'" [Recorded with apologies to Princeton.]

In about 1949, Flossie mused on Betsy's childhood. "It seems strange to think what a 'tomboy' she was on the swing and in the barn and then how feminine she became . . . and still is."

Beth formed half of the cheerleading duo for the girls' basketball team at Southern Boulevard School. Her father maintained that "she swam beautifully, played tennis well, and rode horseback beautifully."

As a fifteen-year-old, she delighted in her adventures at Percy Craw-ford's Christian camp in the Pocono Mountains the summer of 1936. Por-tions of letters home reveal:

> Thursday night, we had a spread. We had a fire down by the lake. We had to be in bed by 10:30, but we never are. The doors here are always open and the nurse here who is in charge won't squeal. Fri-day, we got permission from Percy to have a party and devotions in the woods and come in late. We did.
>
> Mr. Van Horn got Coc and me in a conversation on banking. His advice was, "See the world before you're married." I told him I'd rather see the world with my husband than alone.
>
> I got a permanent. I fell for the man (a Greek, so Mom says) who gave it to me.

Not long afterwards, the self-focused girl changed the direction of her life. Her mother recalled the metamorphosis:

> We are Baptists; but when we moved here, we went to the near-est church, a Methodist in a village nearby. When [our girls were] older, they had no young people's group. So, Beth went to the Presbyterian (the next nearest). A former missionary to China, Dr. Yerkes, was the pastor. From that small group eight missionaries have come forth.
>
> The young people asked Percy Crawford to come one night. We went and that night Beth accepted Christ as her Savior. She was sixteen. The next morning, she came into our room and said, "I am going to be a missionary."
>
> We had allowed her to attend a dancing class, the teacher of whom had very high standards, and also to go to good moving pictures. She at once withdrew from the class (though she loved it) and gave up the "movies." She reasoned that they did her no harm, but might her "brother." Of course, many friends couldn't understand.
>
> In her room was a high bed beside which was a little table and lamp. I can still see her each night, never failing, before going to bed, perched up on that high bed reading her Bible, not from duty; but because to her it was truly a love letter from God to her.
>
> In spite of the narrow path she walked, she had many boy-friends. We were laughing just yesterday—how one boy walked four miles to come see her and would fall asleep on the sofa after he got here. He had four miles to walk home again.

Later, Beth's future husband would share his perspective with his children on her life-changing encounter with God:

> Dr. Yerkes had invited Percy Crawford and his quartet to New Providence Presbyterian Church on a Saturday or Sunday night. Beth wanted to go. Now Florence and Guion were good, respectable church people. But Guion's parents—family—had more real spirituality, the New Birth, etc., than Florence's family. Guion's grandfather was a senior deacon at the First Baptist Church in New York City. But Guion's father moved out to Plainfield.
>
> After Percy Crawford really preached the gospel, Beth immediately went forward. Her father was right there beside her with his arms around her, showing he was all for it, all for it.
>
> Humanly speaking, Beth's getting assurance of salvation and definitely going all out for the Lord was used by God to lead the whole family. That's why Audie [sister Audrey] got converted. And Florence—in her older years, there was nobody like her! Thank the Lord for Dr. Yerkes! I hope all her [Beth's] daughters realize what Beth did for that family. When she got saved, the family didn't influence her; she influenced the family. Of course, she always thought that she was her father's favorite. She said that he admired success and beauty and he thought she was pretty. So, she was the logical one to be the leader.

High school years over, Beth applied to a private two-year girls' school out of state. Her sister Joyce intimated that Beth had selected a distant college to escape her father's smothering ways.

Her mother viewed her choice differently. "Beth chose to go to Stephens College in Missouri. Some of the family thought she should go to a Christian college, as temptations are so great at secular ones. But Beth said her witness could shine brighter at a secular school. I agreed, as I knew she had been truly 'born again' and, though many times she might 'fall down,' she would never fall out."

Beth practiced diligently on the Steinway grand piano in their parlor as she grew up. Her piano teacher confided that Beth had the skill and talent to become a concert pianist. Instead, she chose to serve God on the mission field.

Stephens College boasted a strong Fine Arts Department. There Beth honed her piano skills, while adding harpist to her instrumental repertoire. Her friends wondered how playing a harp could be used in mission work.

But Beth believed that any talent could be used to share Christ if that ability was surrendered to God.

When her first Christmas break rolled around, her father eagerly met her plane. One passenger after another after another descended the stairs. No Beth! Finally, escorted by a flight attendant, she appeared, pea-green from motion sickness.

After completing her two years at Stephens, Beth looked for a four-year college that would prepare her for the mission field. And would "seeing the world with a husband" be part of her future?

Chapter 6

Tall Corn State

1921

U NLIKE Beth Fountain, who grew up on "easy street," Arlene Johanna Jensen faced hardships of cold, want, and death. Parents Bessie and Jens Jensen welcomed her birth on their farm outside Harlan, Iowa, though Jens would have preferred a boy to help with the crops. This blessed fall event occurred 1,200 miles west of New Jersey and five months after Beth's springtime birth.

Arlene Johanna Jensen, ca. mid-1920s.
(Family photo)

Bessie's parents had come from Norway. At age eighteen, Jens immigrated to the USA from Denmark with his sister Christy and their parents. He married Bessie in 1919.

A year later, Bessie's mother died. Then, the next year rheumatic fever stole Jens from his wife and children, leaving Bessie with her older daughter, Margaret, and eight-month-old Arlene. Shortly thereafter, death struck once more, taking Bessie's father.

Jens's parents moved in with the bereaved family. Grandma Jensen knew only Danish, so they all spoke Danish in their home.

Six or seven years later, Mother Bessie promised Arlene a surprise! Then, she introduced her to widower Lars Olsen, Bessie's new husband. Arlene asked, "Where's the surprise?"

As an adult, Arlene insisted, "My stepfather was a very kind man, a sincere Christian loved by many people. On the other hand, he was very much old-country, having emigrated from Denmark."

Tragedy had not bypassed Lars. His first wife, Hulda, had been burning leaves. When her skirt caught fire, she jumped into their farm water tank and drowned.

Lars was twenty-one years older than second wife, Bessie. They birthed a daughter. Lars named her Hulda.

After a time, Jens's parents left to live with their daughter, Christy, and her husband, Rev. Andrew Christopherson.

"Lars was good to Bessie, but he was also opinionated and quite set in his ways." Arlene recalls:

> He did not tell my mother anything of a business nature and never consulted her, nor took her into his confidence. He had a strange attitude toward money. He never gave presents at Christmas or birthdays. We were fortunate if my mother could manage to get us each a dollar gift.
>
> However, if his hogs got a good price on the Omaha market, for example, he would arrive home with a new set of dishes, (which my mother would have loved to choose herself). But then, he had built-in cupboards made in her kitchen in which to keep them. One day, a refrigerator arrived at the back door, a bicycle for me, and a new car. In other words, he was generous, but definitely in his own way.
>
> My mother confided her unhappiness to my older sister, Margaret, who became very nervous and unwell.

Lars spoiled Arlene, his favorite, but was less kind to Margaret or fun-loving Hulda. Arlene said, "I was a demanding child, who could get from my father what I wanted. As a result of my sisters' problems and those I observed with other stepparents, I vowed never to become a stepparent."

Every Sunday, Arlene's aunts, uncles, and cousins came into town for church. Bessie's two sisters, Jessie and Elsie, and their husbands dined at Bessie's. Through the years, Arlene enjoyed her many cousins.

Arlene packed her teen days with activities—school glee club and mixed chorus, debate team (her side lost), and teaching the lower grades her junior and senior years.

She frequented the local library and read avidly, each year keeping a record of books she had read. She favored volumes by Pearl S. Buck, Anne Morrow Lindbergh, and the Christian romance writer Grace Livingston Hill, along with both fiction and nonfiction about nurses, doctors, and missionaries.

At home, she shared the housework—cleaning, ironing, canning, rendering lard, and cooking. Arlene took her turn milking the family cow, churning butter, mowing the lawn, feeding the chickens, and preparing them for the supper pot. She planted and harvested potatoes and carrots and picked cherries and elderberries. Popcorn remained a major food group in her home, as did coffee.

One night, Arlene's stepfather, Lars, invited her to ask Christ into her heart. Of that time she wrote, "I accepted Jesus Christ as my personal Savior and was baptized at nine years of age."

Arlene prioritized church. She taught a children's Sunday school class and summer Bible school, attended Wednesday night prayer meetings, and stayed active in her Baptist Young People's Union. Her peers voted her president her senior high school year. She sang in the church choir and acted in dramatic productions.

Life changed. The middle of March 1938 roared in like a rapacious lion. Arlene deeply loved Lars, the only "Papa" she had ever known. Some-one had given her a zippered ostrich-skin diary that Christmas, in which she wrote:

Wed., Mar. 16, 1938   Papa on special diet.

Tues., Mar 29   Pap sick, has to go to Omaha for operation. Papa packed and ready. Oh dear, what next?

Fri., Apr. 1   Papa operated on . . . Papa fine.

Tues., Apr. 12   Omaha afternoon. Papa blue.

Thurs., Apr. 14   Mama to Omaha. I churned; Margaret washed. Papa quite sleepy.

Sat., Apr. 16   Omaha 11:45. Papa not so good. Poison in his system.

Mon., Apr. 18   Papa awfully bad today. Special nurse 3 p.m. Blood transfusion 9:00. 10:00 all over. He's better off than was before. God help us. Back home 12:00.

Sat., Apr. 23   Twelve men came here, twenty-five altogether—planted potatoes. Most of garden planted.

The farming relatives made sure that there was always food on the bereaved family's table. Arlene's mother sewed all her girls' dresses and crafted exquisite cutwork, embroidering pillow cases, dresser scarves, and tablecloths. Sporadically, she worked outside the home.

Arlene felt especially close to her Aunt Christy and Uncle Andrew Christopherson. They became her spiritual mentors. Besides support from her aunt and uncle, she credits her pastor and his wife (her Sunday school teacher) for her early Christian growth.

Speaking to a young people's mission group decades later, she explained, "I look back on missionary organizations in my church as a very important part of my early life. My church was mission-minded. Many missionaries came to speak. I was always interested in what they said. I had a missionary heroine from my church who was in Assam, India." The Selanders, another missionary couple to India, also told of their work. Laura, their teenage daughter, and Arlene began corresponding with each other. The two would meet again "down the road."

What future lay ahead for Arlene? What dreams did she treasure? "Early, I began to say that I wanted to be a missionary nurse," she revealed. "Though I cannot relate a crisis experience or a specific call as such to be a missionary, the conviction that this was God's purpose for my life never left me, but was strengthened through the years."

Her time at a summer camp at age twelve or older bolstered her heart call for missions. She confided to the same girls' mission group, "When I was sixteen, I went forward one evening to say that I was willing to be a missionary [nurse], if God so led. But just as I was thinking of going to a nursing school, my father died. My mother was left with debts. How could

I go away to school? But God—and I love that phrase—but God opened the way."

Arlene confided to her diary, "Want to be a nurse more than ever."

CHAPTER 7

"L'Étoile du Nord"

1939

ON February 3 and with guidance from Pastor Nelson and his wife, Arlene sent in her application to Mounds-Midway School of Nursing in St. Paul, Minnesota. Three short days later, she wrote, "No news from St. Paul yet." The longed-for missive finally arrived March 11; they accepted her! She would begin her nursing studies in February 1940.

Finishing up her senior high school year, she worked outside the home to earn money for train fare and college expenses. She continued her daily diary thoughts: "Sept. 1, 1939 Hitler declared war 11:30 last night— Oh my!"

Winter hit hard the next year: "Jan. 18, 1940 Twenty-two degrees below this morning. Face and nose nearly frozen. Could see breath. Couldn't get house heated. At 9:30, scooped walks a little at a time. No mail. At 11:00, twenty-four degrees below. Pump all frozen up. Icicles in bathtub. Ice in toilet this morning."

Soon Arlene would exchange the cold of Iowa for winters in Minnesota, known as "the North Star State" or "*L'Étoile du Nord.*"

After years of anticipation, the day to embrace her future finally arrived. She and her friend Annabelle boarded the train for St. Paul on February 7, 1940, nursing school bound! The following day she recorded, "I didn't know anything could be so perfect . . . thrilling to come to hospital! Really here!"

Except for brief visits to friends and family in Harlan, St. Paul would be her home for the next three and a half years. She embraced nursing school avidly. Mounds Park and Midway were two hospital and nursing dormitories across town from each other. She transferred between the two over the years for training and work.

Besides her studies and job on the wards, Arlene forged many friendships among the other students and the town folk, several relationships lasting her entire life. She sampled a variety of churches, often attending a Swedish Baptist church Sunday mornings and others in the evening. At Wednesday night prayer meetings, Arlene enjoyed hearing talks by missionaries. With her school glee club, she sang in churches around the area.

Despite meager finances, she managed to have fun—ice-skating, picnics, swimming, and parties with her pals. David and Esther Blackmore, with their daughter, Virginia, opened their home and hearts to her. They became her surrogate family.

But even roses have thorns. Arlene's supervisor handed her the six-month evaluation form. What a shock! She laid it out in her diary: *"Crisis:* Thurs, Aug. 1 'Read this.' My record—whew! Good constructive criticism. Guess I'm pretty bad. About time I'm getting my eyes opened. Miss Henson swell. Warning me. Little crybaby. Selfish, snippy, always right. Whew! I can take it; I can improve. Nice cry evening. Annabelle swell; big comfort. Time to grow up. What a day!" A few days later, she added, "I will have to get over my bossiness."

Arlene's undergraduate years tortured her with the common angst over boyfriends. One young man, Paul, kissed with style and enthusiasm. And my, did she thoroughly enjoy his kisses! However, he attended dances and movies, which were on the naughty list according to her "Christian check sheet." Their relationship seesawed as season gave way to season.

But in Arlene's March letter to her mother and sisters, she gushed, "Guess I'd better not rave about Albert. You got so worried when I raved about Paul; but suffice it to say that Paul or anyone else I've ever gone with are so far inferior to him, it isn't worth mentioning. Albert is a very beautiful Christian and has a lovely personality."

Albert had his sights set on being a missionary doctor. Arlene wondered if God would lead them together in medical missions. After two pages of writing about Albert, she quipped, "Should I go on talking about Albert or would you rather have me talk about something else for a while?—Ha, Ha!" Alas, even ever-blushing Albert eventually faded into the woodwork and, sadly, no husband peeked over her horizon.

The same could not be said of two of her nursing compatriots. Friends Annabelle and Pinky secretly married two local lads. Had the school discovered their nuptials, the girls would have been expelled for that major infraction. But it didn't and they weren't.

Class work challenged Arlene, especially chemistry. Her studies and required work on the hospital floors wore her down. She experienced frequent medical problems of her own. Her doctor diagnosed numbness on the left side of her face as hyposthenia.

After a year and a half, she was thrilled to graduate out of dark stockings and shoes. "Walking on air; white shoes and hose." She delighted in this mile marker in nursing school. But the pace did not let up. On January 2, 1943, she wrote, "Our only thought is study, dig, dig!" The day after, she admitted, "So tired; slept instead of studying."

At the Swedish Baptist Church, she rededicated her life to God. She reached out to lonely and hurting people. One sick friend closed her letter to Arlene, "From a person who really looks up to you and thinks that you are one of the finest persons with whom I have communicated and one who many people, including myself, think you are about the truest friend that anyone may have except God."

Arlene's family slipped a dollar or more in letters to her. She noted, "Almost $600 in debt—more fun!"

On May 14, she and her classmates swore The Florence Nightingale Pledge. Her older sister Margaret and her husband, Ronald Goodner, young Hulda, and Mom Bessie witnessed her graduation as a registered nurse.

Arlene Jensen, RN. (Photo courtesy of Converge)

Arlene worked for a year at Mounds Park Hospital as a general duty nurse. Then she returned to Iowa to spend time with her mother. There, she employed her skills at the local Harlan hospital. Work demanded time and energy, but she always put church first.

While happy to be with her loved ones, she felt strangely apart. A deep spiritual bond was missing between them. In January 1945, she vented, "I feel that the Lord is calling me to something, whatever it may be. But how can I escape this hopeless financial tangle I'm caught in?"

Arlene wrote about her heart's burden for her fellow hospital workers, that they might find joy and peace in Christ. "What a responsibility it is to live! Oh, God, that I might serve thee to the fullest!"

But God again made a way for her through the financial waves. As World War II ended, veterans under the GI Bill could now afford college. Through the efforts of a congresswoman, Arlene received government Bolton Funds in a new program open to nurses. She enrolled in the University of Minnesota in the health field.

A more mature and disciplined Arlene spent the next two years studying diligently. She plugged into InterVarsity Christian Fellowship and worked with international students.

She continued to have problems with face pain. A complete neurological exam failed to identify the cause.

As part of her nursing school physical fitness, the program had required her to dive into a pool headfirst, despite her fears. For the next ten weeks, numbness blanketed parts of her face. After tests, the doctor diagnosed her with trigeminal neuralgia. That same month, she penned, "Have hyposthenia of trigeminal nerve and cold, so have to go to bed with heat on my face."

Despite this challenge, Arlene was graduated in June of 1948 with a Bachelor of Science in Nursing Education and a certificate in Public Health. Afterward, she taught nursing in her old school, Mounds-Midway.

She admitted, "I still wanted to be a missionary, but . . . where?" Would God open a door for her or leave her lamenting in limbo?

CHAPTER 8

To Eastern Baptist and Beyond!

1939

MERREL Callaway packed his first year at Eastern Baptist Seminary with preaching engagements. He and his friends spoke in prisons and slums. They presented God's claim on lives in churches of several denominations scattered across New England, New Jersey, New York, and Pennsylvania. He squeezed studying into the gaps. When professors assigned his class a chapel service, they chose him to deliver the sermon.

His particular take on Scripture propelled his proclamation: "I had always connected the [Second] Coming of Christ with missions in general. When the body of Christ is complete, then Christ will come in glory for his people. Logically, I thought that the more people get saved, [the sooner Jesus will return]. So, why go to some tribe that has never heard the first time, when you can stay here? For instance, [what if a well-known evangelist is reaching] 100,000 people here, while you're [just] getting entrance to a tribe? So, my enthusiasm was numbers-wise."

Despite this viewpoint, he did join the Student Foreign Missions Fellowship. In time, this organization merged with InterVarsity Christian Fellowship.

After a busy summer, Merrel returned to seminary, not knowing that the trajectory of his life would be changed in two ways. As he and his pal Bill Allen strolled on campus, they spied a new young lady walking around the grounds. They agreed, "Boy, oh boy, the climate is changing around here!"

Beth Fountain had enrolled in Eastern Baptist College. Merrel didn't remember when he and Beth actually met. He did notice her long blond hair as she sat in front of him in a meeting. They both attended the Student Foreign Missions Fellowship. They formed a friendship, which developed and deepened. Beth invited him to spend Christmas with her family in New Jersey and he accepted. By that time, Cupid's arrow had pierced him deeply.

After spending the holiday with the Fountains, Merrel attended the New Jersey Keswick, a missions conference in South Jersey.

Merrel knew well Matthew 24:14 where Jesus explained privately to his chosen disciples, "This gospel of the kingdom shall be preached in all the world for a witness unto all nations; and then shall the end come." He also recalled Mark 13:10: "The gospel must first be published among all nations."

At Keswick he learned that "nations," (*ethne* or *ethnos*) are people groups, persons with like culture and ancestry, with common ethnicity and traditions. "That made a big impression on me," he confided. From that perspective, Christ would come again in majesty and power, not when a certain gazillion people had heard the good news, but when each tribe, language, and people group had been reached with the gospel of God. Unreached ethnic groups, not numbers, became Merrel's lifelong ministry lodestar.

But spring was in the air and this man's fancy already turned to love. Returning to school in January, Merrel sent a note to the Fountains, thanking them for their hospitality. In the letter, he mentioned another young man. He feared that their daughter might be more interested in this other guy than him. He wondered if God permitted this new interest on Beth's part, since Merrel spent so much time thinking about her.

Guion wrote back. He thought that God would want a man to be focused on the woman he desired for his wife. Thus, Merrel knew that Florence and Guion approved of his suit.

He proposed marriage and Beth Fountain accepted. She joined him in Shamokin, Pennsylvania, for revival services. When he mentioned that they had just become engaged, the best jeweler in town brought them to his store. The owner took out a tray with a selection of diamond rings. Beth knew of Merrel's limited finances. She picked out an elegant but modest ring. The Christian businessman sold it to them at a greatly reduced price.

Beth and Merrel pledged their lifelong vows of devotion in June 1941. Merrel wrote of that momentous day:

> We were married at First Baptist Church of Plainfield, NJ, where
> Guion Fountain's family went. All the relatives were in Plainfield,

as well as Beth's best friend. She played the harp. (That was why Beth had learned to play.)

My brother Roy and Papa met the Fountains at the wedding, where Papa prayed. No other Callaways, except Cousin Merrel, Cousin Retta Callaway, and Aunt Vy, were there. Jack Wyrtzen was my best man. As I came out of the vestibule to the altar, who should be sitting right there but Cousin Merrel, who gave me the biggest wink you ever saw!

The reception was at 805 Fairmount Avenue. Cousin Merrel had to get back to NY, but Aunt Vy did come. Roy was embarrassed that she sat there smoking cigarettes. Leave it to Vy!

Some old lady said, "He's really getting a peach, but I don't know what she's getting." When I introduced Beth to Cousin Retta, she said, "You tell 'em to ask Cousin Retta and they'll know what she's getting!"

Elizabeth Fountain Callaway.
(Photo courtesy International Mission Board, SBC)

Of her new son-in-law, Florence Fountain wrote, "I constantly thank God for him; he is so sweet, so full of fun, so consecrated!"

Not ones to waste opportunities for witness, the newlyweds spent their honeymoon traveling from one speaking engagement to another. At these venues, Beth performed on the piano and harp while Merrel preached.

Autumn arrived, along with a new school semester. Beth had already recognized God's summons to mission work at age sixteen. Merrel relates, "It was at seminary that I felt God calling me to be a foreign missionary. This feeling became a conviction as I studied more and more the Bible basis for missions."

Soon the young couple contacted the Southern Baptist Foreign Mission Board, requesting literature about missions. The Board sent them a puzzling response: "We need a couple of the right sort to start an English-speaking church or work opposite the American University of Beirut."

Sensibly they wrote back, "What do you mean, 'of the right sort'?" Dr. Sadler, the Secretary for the Near East, Europe, and Africa, asked to meet them at the Central Railroad Station in Philadelphia on his way back to Virginia from New York City.

Merrel said ironically, "Apparently we were the right sort." Anyway, they then received an invitation to the mission headquarters in Richmond, Virginia. There they learned that an elderly Baptist Lebanese pastor, Said Jureidini, needed assistance in his work in Beirut.

And who was this Jureidini? Born into a Greek Orthodox family in 1866, Mr. Jureidini grew up in a Lebanese mountain village. At that time, Lebanon was part of Syria and ruled by the Ottoman Empire out of Turkey. The conflicting beliefs of Greek Orthodox, Catholic, Protestant, Muslim, and Jew that he encountered confused him. He rebelled against the idea of a God who apparently did nothing to free his country from Ottoman domination. As a young man, he embraced atheism. With an eye for beauty and composition, he opened a photography shop in Beirut.[1]

In 1893, the city of Chicago held a massive fair to celebrate cultural and technological advances made since Christopher Columbus's day. Jureidini's uncle selected his nephew to assist him in setting up the Syrian exhibit in the Turkey building at the Columbus Exhibition.[2]

Said met Christ while in America. A church in Missouri baptized him. He committed his life to God and his service. Returning home, he shared his newfound faith with all he could. When the pastor and deacons from St. Louis visited Lebanon, they commissioned Jureidini as a minister of the

---

1. McRae, *Photographer in Lebanon*, 5, 7, 19, 20.

2. McRae, *Photographer in Lebanon*, 22.

gospel. Said then baptized the eight men he had led to Christ.[3] They formed the first Baptist church in Lebanon.[4]

Between 1905 and 1925, the General Association of Baptist Churches in Illinois supported him sporadically. Said's faithful band of Lebanese believers grew and birthed churches in other towns.[5] In 1927, the Southern Baptist Convention accepted him as their missionary to Lebanon. Devout Christians there hoped that workers from America would be sent to share their task of evangelizing Lebanon for Christ.[6] But during World War II, the Foreign Mission Board had no clue how their money was being spent. They hoped that Merrel and Beth would go there to report on and oversee finances, wanting to be good stewards of God's money. The Callaways were also to assist Pastor Jureidini in his work.

Someone asked Merrel later if he had really been committed to work among Arabs or in Beirut at that time. He confessed, "No, I had to look it up. There's a German city, Bayruth [in Bavaria]. I had to look it up on a map to see where Beirut, Lebanon, really was."

3. McRae, *Photographer in Lebanon*, 33–39.

4. Trexler, *Evangelizing Lebanon*.

5. McRae, *Photographer in Lebanon*, 48–50.

6. McRae, *Photographer in Lebanon*, 59.

CHAPTER 9

God's Timing

1941

O N December 7, the United States of America plunged into World War II. Five months later, Beth earned her Bachelor of Arts degree and Merrel a Masters of Divinity. In August of 1942, Beth's parents and Merrel's father and sister Gyp met the graduates at Ridgecrest, a Southern Baptist conference center in North Carolina.

Beth's father, Guion, sent a Western Union telegram to daughters Joyce and Audrey: "Betsey and Merrel appointed missionaries by the Southern Baptist Mission Board."

With the war in full swing, the Board put overseas plans on hold. At its expense, the appointees attended Harvard University in Boston, Massachusetts. There they immersed themselves in Arabic, the history of Arabia, and Islam to prepare themselves for their work ahead. Beth went to sister school Radcliff for most of her classes.

Kate Ellen Gruver and Beth Callaway, "under appointment to Beirut, Syria; Harvard Divinity School in background," 1944. (Photo courtesy of International Mission Board, SBC)

Merrel's father said:

> Looks as if this kid will never finish schooling, as he has been at it
> since six years of age. He sho' ought to be prepared for something
> by now. Personally, there were mixed feelings of gladness and sad-
> ness when I learned that the Board had accepted the young people
> and I am sure the Fountains felt the same. At my life's expectancy,
> I cannot expect to see them often before the Lord calls me home;
> but I'd rather have them in Syria in the Lord's will than have them
> here out of it.

At a missions conference at Gordon College of Theology and Missions, the famed Apostle to Islam, Samuel Zwemer, presented a lecture.
Afterward, by mail Merrel requested an interview with him. He describes
their meeting at Dr. Zwemer's hotel in New York City:

> Zwemer was sold on literature, having written fifty books and lots
> of gospel tracts. He came down the elevator, while I was sitting
> in the lobby. So, typical Zwemer, instead of coming to find me,
> Zwemer went over to the news stand, bought a paper, and gave
> the guy a gospel tract. Then he came over to me and we talked. He
> asked, "What are you going to do?"
> After about fifteen minutes of my talking about going to Leb-
> anon, he said, "But have you ever thought of a place like Arabia,
> so neglected?"
> Then I talked more about my plans for Lebanon. He [coun-
> tered], "But, you know, you Southern Baptists have the evange-
> listic zeal, you've got the numbers, you've got the big money, the
> ability and stick-to-itiveness, and you've got what it takes to do
> something about those unreached countries." And he just kept on.

Decades later, Merrel said, "People don't realize it, but that was the
crucial point of God getting the Southern Baptists to turn to Arabia. Hu-
manly speaking, it was Samuel Zwemer whom God used to get Southern
Baptists into Bahrain and finally into Yemen. So, we owe a lot to Samuel
Zwemer."

While at Harvard and Radcliffe, Merrel and Beth met a young Jewish
lady. She became a Christian, much to her well-educated parents' horror.
Merrel mentioned, "She said she [accepted Christ as her Messiah] because
of what she saw in Beth and in our Christian marriage; she saw Jesus." The
two of them would meet again over a decade later.

As the year in Boston wound down, InterVarsity offered Merrel the position of staff member for New England. And his friend Jack Wyrtzen recommended him for a pastorate in Worcester, Massachusetts.

Merrel also described how each morning in their Harvard apartment, he and Beth were awakened by the tramping of three hundred ordained ministers, many with potbellies, training to be chaplains in the military. "Their main purpose at Harvard," Merrel pointed out, "was to learn how to read a map in case they got lost in a forest or something. With them right under our noses, I began to wonder, 'Is that why God brought us to Harvard? Does he want me to go in the chaplaincy?'"

Merrel wrote the Mission Board about these three job possibilities. The Board responded equably: "These are all good things. You mentioned a pastorate. The Women's Missionary Union of Virginia is willing to take your full support to organize a Baptist church in Alexander Park, VA, not too far from the Norfolk Navy Yard in Portsmouth, VA. There will be 5,000 new houses and 2,000 trailers. There are no schools, no churches, no nothing."

The government moved workers in by the thousands near the Navy Yard to support the war effort. Beth and Merrel agreed that this was God's best for them at that time. They moved to Virginia until the door to Beirut would open.

"We discovered that people didn't know how to find our church," Merrel stated. "We decided to get a radio program to inform them that the services were in the auditorium of a new elementary school. The choir and I went to the radio studio on Saturday and Sunday nights. I preached a short message and gave directions to the church. Beth played the piano as the choir sang."

The Callaways expected their first child in January 1944. That year, the song "Mairzy Doats"[1] captivated the country. Merrel said that on the night of their daughter's birth, "All America was singing 'Mairzy Doats.' In the hospital, doctors were humming it, nurses singing it, and radios blaring 'Mairzy Doats.'"

Dark-haired Baby Sharon made her entrance early Sunday morning. The next evening, Merrel informed his radio audience, "You might be interested to know that the young lady who plays the piano for this program presented me with a beautiful baby girl after midnight last night at King's Daughter's Hospital."

1. Al Hoffman, *"Mairzy Doates."*

The following day, Merrel attended the Baptist Ministers' Conference. "When I arrived," he abashedly admits, "they were ready for me. They asked, 'Merrel, who was that young lady you were talking about who presented you with that baby? Do you even know her name?'" The new father had failed to mention that the baby's mother was his wife!

Merrel added, "One of those tormentors was John Wilcox, pastor of a fast-growing church in Norfolk. He had a deacon from Chicago. When the deacon went back to his home church and discovered that they were without a pastor, he recommended Wilcox." John accepted the position. He and Merrel reconnected years later.

The Callaways ministered to their community, with many coming to know Christ as Savior. One man identified Merrel as the individual who most impacted his life. "Many years ago," George Presson recalled, "Merrel sat down on an old wooden couch with me in the back room and took his Bible and led me to Christ." He said that Pastor Callaway showed up one snowy day for church, despite a badly injured leg and preached to them.[2] Sixty years in the future, another gentleman told Merrel's third daughter how he had accepted Jesus Christ through Merrel's personal contact.

Alexander Park Baptist Church developed through the years into a strong, godly ministry, sending many servants of God throughout the United States and abroad. In the late forties, a group of young businesswomen at Melrose Baptist Church in Roanoke formed a missions circle. They named their organization after Beth. In 1998, they were "Celebrating 50 Years of Service in His Name . . . Beth Callaway Women on Mission."

But Beth agonized over her sister Joyce's spiritual condition. "One morning," Merrel recounted, "I gave the teaching on 'The Sterner Aspects of God's Love.'" He emphasized that, while an all-powerful, loving God sacrificed himself to offer us eternal life, a holy God cannot look upon sin. If we reject his costly gift of salvation, an eternity of separation from him results.

After the service, Merrel returned to the parsonage. His wife sobbed on her knees beside the bed, distraught and worried that her beloved sister might be facing eternal punishment. Through the rest of her life, Beth continued to be burdened for Joyce's salvation.

In the summer, Merrel's adored mother, Rosalind Valerie Royall Callaway of James Island, South Carolina, passed away at Fernandina Beach,

---

2. Presson in telephone conversation with Susan Callaway Anderson in March 2001.

Florida. On the way to the cemetery, her husband told his youngest, "Mama didn't have a selfish bone in her body."

The Foreign Mission Board vowed to get the Callaways to the Middle East as soon as feasible. In late spring of 1945, a flotilla of thirteen US naval vessels would sail for the European/North African theaters. The military agreed to take a limited number of civilians on board. The trio of Callaways secured passage on a troop ship—Merrel's second crossing of the Atlantic in wartime.

CHAPTER 10

"Over the Bounding Main"

1945

As the troop ship churned past the Statue of Liberty, "The Star-Spangled Banner" boomed over the loud speaker. Beth and Merrel assumed it was in honor of the French lady. However, the captain confided that the Germans had finally surrendered. Victory in Europe had been declared!

Civilians on the ship included Dr. Yerkes's daughter and her husband. He planned to teach at the Biblical Seminary of Yoknow in India. Dr. Bideau, president of the American University of Cairo, taught Merrel an important Arabic word—"*imshi*," meaning "get," "go away."

The menfolk bunked in the craft's underbelly. The women enjoyed nicer quarters. The ship's doctor graciously allowed women with young children to sleep in the empty sick bay at night. He shared some of the ship's milk and other supplies with the little ones. The Hagoods—Henry, Julia, and toddler Jimmy—were also Baptists bound for Palestine. Julia, a lively redheaded Texas farm girl, remembered after sixty years her cabin-sharing experience. "There were only two chairs in our room; Beth draped her dresses over both of them." Oops!

According to Merrel, "Three civilian wives on board were Presbyterian. One belonged to the denomination Presbyterian USA, another the United Presbyterians. The third claimed Carl McIntyre's split-off branch. So, we called them 'the P's,' 'the U-P's,' and 'the Split Peas.'"

Beth wrote home:

> Since we are not supposed to date these letters, I shan't . . . This is a French crew. Our cabin steward doesn't speak a word of English and our waiter only a little. We have to wear [life belts] all the

time. It's some job to carry a life belt and Sharon and hers as well. They've made a tiny one for her.

Merrel is in a cabin with one hundred men, three tiers deep. His bed is just a piece of canvas, like the soldiers. Sharon and I are with three other females and their offspring. Needless to say, we have a hectic time of it. Sharon will just get to sleep, when Jimmy will start to cry and wake her. Then we finally get them quiet, when Harvey arrives and wakes them, and on infinitum. . . . Four times the little monkey [Sharon] has wriggled out of her bag and come walking out the hall, hollering, "Daddy, Daddy!" She did it one night at 2:30 a.m. She sleeps in the bottom bunk and I in the top. I heard this chatter on the floor and there was Miss Sharon.

We share a suite and bath with three other ladies, two babies each eight months old, and four children under five. They all holler day and night. We have water only from six to seven a.m. and five-thirty to six-thirty p.m. It's difficult to get the babies and their clothes washed with so many folks sharing the water in the basin for two hours. (I'm at dinner one half-hour of the time.)

I'm not at all seasick on smooth days, but let it get a little rough and I'm out like a light. "Mothersill's" [seasick] pills are of no avail. . . . We have to go slowly because of so many ships. We are supposed to pass Gibraltar at four a.m. tonight.

Sharon gets as dirty as a pig, but I can't help it. She is now sitting on a lady's life-preserver, bouncing up and down. She's quite a pet on the boat. Each night at six-thirty we have a hymn singing and devotional on deck. Sharon is hitting on all sixes, as usual. Her harness and raps are coming in handy.

Next, Merrel told of his life with the military convoy:

There was a lot of target practice, shooting of guns; because they were afraid that some German U-boat would not have heard that the war was over and torpedo us. For the same reason, we had nightly blackouts on the boat.

Sharon, a toddler, was the darling of all 3,000 GIs. They were also the enemy, as they tossed their cigarette butts into the gutters along the deck. I wanted to sit by the cabin on a nice bench to enjoy the sea air. Sharon went for those hundreds of butts. I put a harness on her. As I sat on a bench on one side of the deck, I held the rope tightly enough to keep her from reaching the temptingly inviting butts as they floated in the gutter.

Every afternoon at sunset, the chaplain would ask three of us to come out on the poop deck. Maybe 250 or 300 soldiers would gather out in the open air. One of the soldiers played the portable pump organ, which could be folded up to resemble a large suit-case, complete with handle. He would start off playing popular songs. Then he would move to well-known hymns, like "The Old Rugged Cross."[1]

Each of us missionaries could only speak for three minutes, which was hard on me. The chaplain asked us to tell what we would say to a wounded man who had only three minutes to live. It was a real challenge, but a wonderful opportunity. One Sunday morning, the Yerkes's daughter and her husband, another person, and I formed a quartet and sang, "The Love of God."[2] Beth played the organ, I think.

Merrel received a thought-provoking lesson from a follower of Islam. "I was sitting on the lower deck with my Bible on the rail beside me. A Muslim fellow came up and said, 'You Christians obviously don't think much of your religious book, because you're sitting beside it. A Muslim treats the Qur'an with much more respect than to have it at the same level as his backside!'"

"I prayed for North Africa for the first time," Merrel revealed, "the night we got in the Mediterranean Sea." The ship passed Morocco and Algeria before docking in Tunis, Tunisia, where some soldiers disembarked:

We woke up that morning and there we were in the harbor with all those sunken ships. In the early sunlight I asked a guy, "Could I climb down the rope ladder just to say I had put my foot on North African soil?" (I didn't dream that I myself would someday be identified with North Africa.) He let me and I climbed down and back up again. He knew I was one of those crazy Americans.

The ship churned into Port Said, Egypt, to let off civilians before resuming its journey to the Pacific. The Callaway and Hagood parents with their small children searched for a place to spend the night. In the morning, they planned to board a train for Palestine. The word "*imshi*" proved useful in warding off marauding beggars. The couples finally asked a young man for a good hotel. He knew just the place that Americans liked to frequent. In the dark of evening, the tired travelers knocked on the door of an establishment. A madame peeked out, cased the weary families, then started shrieking in Arabic at their guide, "Go away! Go away!" He had led them to a brothel! They found other accommodations.

---

1. Bennard, "The Old Rugged Cross." In the public domain.
2. Lehman, "The Love of God." In the public domain.

A train took them the following day across the Sinai Peninsula, through Western Palestine, and up the hills to Jerusalem—their temporary home for language study.

But all was not well in the "City of Peace."

CHAPTER 11

Hills of Zion
and Mountains of Lebanon

1945

THE four adults plunged into Arabic studies at the Newman School of Missions. The Hagoods settled into the Baptist Mission House on Henrietta Szold Street (later renamed Narkis Street.)[1] The Callaways boarded at the American Colony hostel. Their large room appeared Oriental in style. Its tile floor sported a flower motif. The yellow and pink stone buildings sheltered a courtyard with a gurgling fountain.

Horatio Spafford, who penned "It Is Well with My Soul,"[2] had led a group in August of 1881 to live in Jerusalem.[3] In the late 1950s, their settlement building became a hotel. At the time the Callaways lived there, Horatio's daughter Bertha Spafford Vestor managed the property. She had placed her father's Bible in the library. Scripture was printed on the left pages and lines on the right. In Merrel's travels, he had lost his sermon notes. He made the manager an offer for *The Blank-Paged Bible*.[4] Vestor agreed.

Besides intense language study, Merrel preached Sundays at the Mission Church. Henry took the Wednesday night service. He drove to Nazareth each weekend to start their work there.

---

1. Mullican Jr. and Tournage, *One Foot in Heaven*, 88.

2. Spafford, "It Is Well with My Soul," 1873. In the public domain. See Geniesse, *American Priestess*, 63–65.

3. Geniesse, *American Priestess*, 84–90.

4. *The Blank-Paged Bible*.

Eventually, Merrel and Beth squeezed in sightseeing. They encountered Orthodox Jewish boys and men with locks of hair hanging from their temples, Muslim women draped in black veils, Arabs astride donkeys, and herds of goats crowding the streets.

They visited the Mount of Olives and the Tomb of the Kings with about fifty sepulchers chiseled of solid rock in the first century AD. By the tomb rested a massive rolling stone, shaped like a huge, thick coin. This could be rolled in a groove down to the entrance.

At the Palestine Potteries, craftsmen made the famous Jerusalem tiles. Muslims brought Armenians to Jerusalem to make the bright blue tiles which adorn the Dome of the Rock, the site of Solomon's Temple. The family watched the potter fashion the clay with his bare hands as it spun around. He could mold a beautiful vase in two minutes if the clay was not lumpy. There was a room for slightly defective pottery, which were called "castaways." Instead of being sold at low prices, these castaways remained on the shelves, collecting dust. The apostle Paul's words came to the missionaries' minds: "I keep under my body, and bring it into subjection: lest that by any means, when I have preached to others, I myself should be a castaway" (1 Corinthians 9:27).

"Last Thursday was the King of England's birthday parade," Merrel and Beth wrote. "Veterans from Sicily and North African campaigns, as well as others, took part. There were planes, tanks, guns on wheels, men on horses, camels galore, and two Scottish bagpipe bands from the Highlands of Scotland . . . Aside from these exciting things, our life is spent in Arabic and more Arabic."

The Hagoods and Callaways traveled together to Lebanon. As they left Jerusalem, they watched hundreds of Jews file slowly to the Wailing Wall, the only remaining part of the Second Jewish Temple. The day was the ninth of Av, the day on which Titus destroyed the Temple in AD 70.

The two families travelled to Beirut, a 350-mile journey north. There, they finally met Pastor Said Jureidini. They would assess what remained of Baptist work in Lebanon after the war.

Map pf the Levant, 1946
(Courtesy of Steve McCord, Manager of Analysis and Reporting, and Jim McCord,
Senior GIS Analyst, International Mission Board, SBC)

The families stayed in Pastor Jureidini's Mission House, across the street from the American University of Beirut. The school perched on a hill overlooking the blue Mediterranean, snow-capped mountains towering in the distance.

The new missionary couples received a blessing from Rev. Jureidini. God had raised up Salem Sharoud to help him in his work. Salem spoke no English, so the Americans conversed with him in sign language. Beth enthused over their host:

> Mr. J. is a dear old man and loves babies. When he saw our baby, he just cried. He wants Sharon to call him, "*Juddi*," "grandfather." A neighboring preacher asked Merrel to preach for him, but Bro. J. flatly refused, saying, "I've waited three years for this boy to come and I'm not going to let him out of my sight!"
>
> Bro. J. is stone deaf and extremely feeble. He is only able to preach for five minutes now. This house is built around a huge center hall [a *dar*] in which services are held, with pews, organ, and pulpit. Only pay $10.00 per month for rent. Hard to live with a

church in the middle of your home. Sunday School is at 10:30 and folk begin coming at 8:30!

Sharon is really flourishing here. She greets all the church members with a handshake and says, "How do?" She had a bad fever from mosquito bites. Malaria runs rampant here and we were worried. But she soon recovered.

Sharon also received her first offer of marriage. An Arab couple, the Towils, have a five-year-old son. Mr. T. suggested, "Why don't you promise Sharon as a bride to Musa? We'll start paying for her now."

The Callaways found Beirut ugly, dirty, and dingy, with narrow streets. Nevertheless, they preferred it to cleaner, newer Jerusalem. It had a certain life, more of a big city atmosphere than Jerusalem had. The heat, though, was unbearable.

Beth and Julia Hagood began their missionary work with a vengeance. Beth explained:

Bro. J. has a seven-room house. He has been living here alone for several years. The kitchen is a sight! Primitive conveniences (or lack of them). We females are supposed to do the cooking and are about ready to tear our hair out. Two little oil affairs to cook on and they blow out every five minutes; it takes a half-hour to relight them. This is surely "Life in the Raw!"

We finally engaged a woman to clean away some of the debris. Upon her arrival, Mr. J. said that we were out of water for the next few days and no cleaning could be done!

The two husbands trundled up the mountains to the village of Kefr Mishky, to see more ongoing Baptist work. Nadeen, a consecrated Arab, preached there. Merrel planned to ordain him on their next trip to the village. Henry and Merrel traveled four hours on a rickety bus, then rode donkeys the next hour and a half. Merrel got so sore that he finally slid off and walked. Upon arriving, he drank six cups of thick coffee. Apparently, there's a trick to refusing another cup. One must tilt the cup a certain way to show that you are truly finished. Merrel figured that his hand probably shook so badly after all that caffeine that the host thought he was finished. A nice juicy fly surfaced in his last cup.

About Lebanon, Merrel shared:

The people and clothing are strange, but the services are like those in South Georgia country churches . . . At the church in the mountains where I preached, there were no musical instruments and only three songbooks, but we had an enjoyable service with about fifty people present. When I said the first word in English, some boys in the front row burst into giggling before the elders could check the flood of amusement. After that, they were very reverent.

The six returned to Jerusalem, the adults for language tasks.

Merrel's father, T.W., sent out letters from time to time, which he addressed to the CCC (Children of the Callaway Clan). In them, he quoted from the missionaries' letters. Then he injected his own pithy comments in parentheses:

> Merrel: "This Arabic language and my preaching have kept my nose pretty close to the grindstone."
>
> T.W.: (He doesn't say a word about helping his poor wife with that baby. Just like a preacher!)
>
> Beth: "Sharon does a good job in getting her father out of bed. She brings his shoes and socks to him and stands there pulling until he gets out of bed and puts them on. However, I want you to have your son take a course in Domestic Science. He will not cook, wash dishes, sweep, hang out baby clothes, but just wants to sit around and read lives of great missionaries."
>
> T.W.: (Maybe he hopes to be one someday, but never until he knows how to help his wife. Who would have thought I'd rear a boy who wouldn't take all these burdens off his wife!)

Despite their busy lives, the Callaways prayed for the hundreds of American soldiers to whom they had witnessed or preached on the troop transport.

While in Beersheba, Beth observed that some married women wore a string of silver coins around their foreheads and faces. In that culture, a bridegroom presented these coins to his bride. If she lost one of them, it meant that she had been unfaithful to her husband once—unfaithful twice if she loses two, and so on. Some say that that is why the woman in Luke 15:8–9, when she lost the coin, searched frantically for it before her husband returned home. When she found it, she called her women friends to rejoice with her.

The town of Beersheba lay about fifty miles south of Jerusalem, near the Sinai Desert and Arabia. Black Bedouin tents surrounded the village, which consisted mostly of mud huts. Many women wore embroidered traditional dresses and head scarves. Around their foreheads gleamed three rows of coins. From the center of the forehead, more coins extended over the nose and down to the chin. Yet another strand tied this piece around the neck.

The Callaways moved to Beirut in September. Merrel took over the Sunday and Wednesday night preaching at those services. He recalls, "The first Sunday, I was there in a room full of Baptist men in one of their homes. I was sitting on a divan [with legs stretched out]. Someone told me later that it was very, very impolite to sit like this with the soles of my feet facing toward [others]. If you really lose your temper, you take off your shoe and wiggle the sole; boy, that's terrible!"

Beth's piano playing drew students from the university across the street. Then her husband shared the gospel.

From physically feeble Said Jureidini, Merrel learned much both culturally and spiritually:

> Recently, he told me something which throws light on the verse, "No man, having put his hand to the plough, and looking back is fit for the kingdom of God" (Luke 9:62). He said that, as a young man, on leaving home for the first time, he heard his mother call to him, "Look back, Said, or you'll never return to me." That belief was common in this area for generations. So, the Scripture must mean that the one who looks back to the things of the world, after claiming to be a follower of Christ, will return to his old ways—is not sincere.
>
> He also says that when an Arab boy is chasing another with threats and a bystander says in Arabic, "You will bite his heel," it means, "You can do nothing to him," or, as we would say, "You will bite the dust." The meaning of this Semitic phrase is interesting in view of Gen. 3:15, which says that "the seed of the woman will bruise the serpent's (Satan's) head and the serpent will bruise his heel." In other words, Satan will bite the dust in trying to touch Christ and frustrate God's purpose in him.
>
> Mr. J. also says that in his boyhood days, most men of real wealth and exalted position had a cloakroom with full-length capes or long robes for anyone who might be invited into their presence for a meal or otherwise. There were garments for all, free of charge, and it was a mark of disrespect to come into the nobleman's banquet room without one of these full-length garments. It explains Matt. 22:11–13, where the king came in to see the guests and "saw there a man who had not on a wedding garment. And he saith unto him, 'Friend, how camest thou in hither not having a wedding garment?' And he was speechless. Then the king said to

his servants, 'Bind him hand and foot, and take him away, and cast him into outer darkness.'" There is no excuse for anyone to show disrespect for the King-Christ by trying to come into his presence without being covered with the robe of Christ's righteousness; because the King has provided ample wedding garments for all.

Having assessed the situation in Lebanon for several months, the family returned to Jerusalem in late December. They had lived at the relatively safe American Colony hostel. Now they moved to the YMCA. An empty picture frame hung on one wall. Underneath, the words proclaimed, *Whom Not Having Seen, We Love.*

Julia, Henry, and Jimmy moved to their work in Nazareth.

On January 4, Merrel, Henry, and two other Baptist missionaries, Kate Ellen Gruver and Bob Lindsey, gathered for an executive mission meeting. Henry felt poorly, so they met in his home. The next day, the other three learned that James Henry Hagood had died of a heart attack. Shocked and saddened, Merrel and Bob Lindsey conducted Henry's homegoing service the following day.

Newly widowed, Julia Hagood, with Kate Ellen Gruver, began a Home for Orphans in Nazareth.

On a somewhat happier note, the Callaways attended an engagement ceremony for two workers in the mission. Engagements in Palestine bound couples securely and were seldom broken. Families still chose their offspring's mates. But these two national Christians fell in love and decided to marry. The man's family refused to have anything to do with his prospective bride. While they had nothing against her, they were furious that their son had chosen his own wife.

Merrel never forgot one night in summer of 1946. He and Beth expected their second child soon. Beth told him it was time to call the doctor. As they waited for their taxi to arrive to take them to the hospital, the next-door neighbor's shortwave radio blared that all-too-familiar song, "Mairzy Doats." Through the years, Merrel insisted, "Every time I hear that song that was all the rage when Sharon was born, I nearly have a heart attack!" Susan safely emerged to her new world and her father survived, too.

Less than a month later, though, many others did not survive.

CHAPTER 12

Salam/Shalom—
Where There Is No Peace

1946

T HE Irgun, a Jewish terrorist organization, bombed the massive King David Hotel on Monday, July 22. British military had been using part of the hotel as their headquarters for their Protectorate over Palestine.[1] The Zionist organization allegedly warned of the attack, though the facts are disputed.[2] Merrel gravely recorded his perspective on life in the Holy City:

> Our home was close enough to the King David Hotel for the ex-plosion to rock a huge wardrobe back and forth in our bedroom. Beth was lying on the bed near the wardrobe when the bomb ex-ploded. Our grammar teacher's daughter was killed and the other seriously injured. A British official, who attended our language school and with whom I had attended a social function just a few nights previously, was killed. Another language teacher, an Arab lady, who taught him, had talked with the fellow about his soul's welfare and had given him a New Testament and some gospel tracts just a few days before the explosion.
>
> Bombings seem to be about all the news from Jerusalem now. There was another last night and one this afternoon, which de-molished the front rooms of the Income Tax building. A friend of mine found some old tax returns of some personal friends. The papers were floating down to the earth when she grabbed them and noticed what they were. But a soldier took them from her

---

1. Kramer, *A History of Palestine*, 305.
2. Bruce Hoffman, "The Bombing, July 1946," 594-611.

before she had time to take them away from the ruins and torture her friends with some of the facts on their returns.

Last Wednesday night, while waiting for an approaching bus, which was to take me to a prayer meeting, I heard a tremendous blast and saw a huge flash of light. The terrorists had bombed a British army vehicle full of soldiers and glass started falling all around me. Only a moment before I had walked within three feet of the bomb, not knowing that it was there. But although the soldiers were seriously injured, nothing hit me, though I was completely exposed on the sidewalk. A girl four times further from the bomb than I was knocked to the ground by the concussion.

Although windows were shattered on the two floors beneath our room, our glass was not broken. We are thankful for that, because my wife was standing at our window at that moment. She saw the flash and heard the explosion. After a moment, she began to quiet a girl who happened to be in the room and who had just a few months before been dug from the ruins of the King David Hotel.

After assuring the girl that everything was safe, Beth remembered that her own husband must have been at the scene of the explosion. So, she "let out" a scream that put those of the girl to shame and ran into the street, through broken glass, tree limbs, and stumps, to the bus which I had planned to take. The passengers said that there was no Callaway on the bus.

One of them, a policeman's wife, in sympathy with Beth, told her that she and her husband had been enjoying some sightseeing on the first holiday he had had for four months. "And now," she complained, "the windows of our bus are broken by a bomb and my husband has to go back to work immediately—a real busman's holiday!"

After listening to these words of sympathy with great patience, Beth continued her search for me. And I am happy and thankful to say that she found me all in one piece.

These otherwise tragic incidences had assured us that, if the Lord can protect us within three feet of an unexploded bomb, then he can protect and care for us anywhere he chooses.

And God had not forgotten Julia and Jimmy Hagood either. The orphanage in Nazareth that she and Kate Ellen had begun was going well. As they had secured extra help, Kate Ellen encouraged Julia to resume her Arabic studies for three months. Jimmy and Julia settled again into Jerusalem in early April. Her work at the orphanage had grown her vocabulary, but her grammar suffered. A classmate, Finlay Graham, kindly began tutoring her in the afternoons.

Finlay had served in the Middle East in the British Royal Air Force during the recent war. He had felt led by God to return to the area as a missionary, though he had no mission support. A friendship developed between the two students.

Finlay told Merrel about a British fellow, Dr. Charles McLean, who had a hospital in Trans-Jordan (or Jordan) called the Gilead Mission Trust. The hospital had been built mainly on his wife's family money. But the ministry suffered from inheritance taxes. Amazingly, the Callaways sent Dr. McLean $100 for his work. "That small (but for me, large) gift to a perfect stranger marked the beginning of a friendship which they renewed two years later . . . in a way that only God could dream up, much less plan!"

Beth and Merrel also slipped $25 to an author who was struggling with writer's block. In her discouragement, she almost gave up her efforts. But the Holy Spirit undergirded her and she became a noted author. Hannah Hurnard's well-known allegory *Hind's Feet on High Places*[3] sustained a Callaway daughter decades later through two dark episodes in her life.

During the years in Palestine and Lebanon, the Callaways became more and more burdened for the millions in Arabia who had not heard of Christ's love for them. The two requested of the Board that they be allowed to pioneer in that vast land. The very next day, they saw a copy of a convention address given by the Women's Missionary Union president, a Mrs. Martin. She made a strong plea for work to be started in Arabia. After the arrival of the Callaways' letter in the States, the Board's literature was full of information about Arabia. Word from Dr. Sadler, their area secretary, expressed his complete willingness for their proposed venture, put the crowning seal of approval on the move.

Merrel and Beth contacted their supporters. "Perhaps you wonder how we can think of leaving Lebanon. The answer is that millions of people in Arabia have practically no witness. Only one mission working on the eastern fringe has seriously tried to tackle that area, which has been closed, not only to missionaries, but to foreigners as well. Our group in Lebanon is on the way to becoming indigenous, self-supporting; and we feel that our services are needed more in Arabia . . . 'Go ye, therefore, and *teach all nations*'" [Matthew 28:19].

---

3. Hurnard, *Hinds' Feet on High Places*.

Merrel applied for a visa to explore the possibility of opening work in the Hadramaut area or in Yemen in the Southern Arabian Peninsula. Authorities denied him entry. "Twenty years later," he said, "they told me that the reason we'd been turned down then was that 'there hadn't been a Christian in Yemen on over thirteen hundred years and we weren't about to let one in then.'"

All was not lost, however. Ida Patterson had been a Southern Baptist missionary in China. When she came home on furlough, she met the Callaways in Virginia. There also she got to know a medical missionary, Dr. Harold Storm. He worked on the island of Bahrain off the east coast of Arabia. Storm's wife had drowned in the Persian Gulf, leaving him with a young boy and girl. Ida and Harold forged a friendship. Merrel described the Storm-Patterson engagement: "He said, 'Wilt thou?' and she wilted." So, Ida joined the Reformed Church of America and went to Bahrain with her new husband.

When the Storms heard that the Callaways had been refused entry to Yemen and the Hadramaut, Ida and Harold invited them to come to Bahrain. The Storms planned to furlough for a year. Another couple, Dr. and Mrs. Harrison, would be gone the following year. The Storms and Harrisons offered their houses to the Callaways. Merrel and Beth hoped to use Bahrain as a springboard to access Yemen in Southwest Arabia and the Hadramaut in South Central Arabia. The Southern Baptist Foreign Mission Board approved this venture, though Merrel and Beth still had months of language study ahead.

They felt God leading them to begin weeks of evangelistic meetings in Jerusalem. Christians of many denominations first joined in three weeks of prayer for Palestine. They handed out about a thousand gospels of John. Soldiers from England, Australia, and Canada came to the services, along with several Scottish fellows in their kilts. Unfortunately, authorities had cordoned off several areas of the city due to increased violence, so fewer Arabs could attend.

"The soldiers all had to carry their guns into the service," Beth explained, "and there was much rattling and clanging of the artillery, but nobody minded. Occasionally, a gun would drop on the floor and what a bang it would make!"

She detailed apparent efforts by the forces of evil to oppose their work:

> The devil has struck in so many ways, one of which is the attempt
> to weaken the bodies of those taking part in the preaching, music,

etc. We found it terribly hard to keep going physically. Each night, we have an organ, piano, and accordion and those who play them feel weighted down, as though we couldn't play another note. Merrel, who has been doing the preaching, has a bad cold, has been unable to sleep, and has generally had the "wrung-out dishrag" feeling.

We have put a huge sign advertising the meetings outside our window and the devil seem after that, too. One night, a terrific windstorm arose, unheard of here at this time of year. It nearly tore the sign up. Merrel had to go out in his nightclothes to bring it in. Immediately the sign got in, the wind ceased. The next day, both ropes holding it broke and fell, barely missing hitting a man on the head.

Despite this opposition, thirty-five soldiers found Christ. One testified, "Tuesday night, I accepted Christ as my Savior, but went back to the barracks with some questions still in my mind about it all. It just seemed too simple. But the next day, I took time alone to have my first prayer meeting with the Lord and since then I know I'm saved."

Though some had found peace with God in their hearts, others did not. The violence in Palestine escalated in 1947. While the majority of the population was Arab, the traumatized Jews from Europe and across the world tried feverishly to pour into the land.

CHAPTER 13

Destruction

1947

D ECEIT by the Allied Powers in World War I set the stage for disaster. At that time, the Ottoman Empire ruled parts of the Middle East, including Palestine. The British virtually promised the Arabs self-determination if the Arabs would help them defeat the Ottomans, who were aligned with the Central Powers.[1] Against this, the secret 1916 Sykes–Picot Agreement laid the groundwork for Britain, Russia, and France to carve up the Middle East into its own colonies or "protectorates."[2] Then in 1917, British Lord Balfour penned what became known as the Balfour Declaration, promising the Jews a homeland within Palestine.[3]

By 1920, France and Britain "protected" much of the Middle East. But after fighting for the Allies, the Arabs wanted self-determination for their land, where their ancestors had lived for millennia. The Jews also wanted a country of their own finally, where their people had lived two thousand years previously. Neither wanted the existing British protectorate.

At 3:30 p.m. on March 1, 1947, Merrel witnessed destruction and death at the Goldsmith Officers' Club on King George Street:

> By this time, we were staying at the Assemblies of God guesthouse. We lived in one bedroom. I had visited the Goldsmith Club, which was on the other side of the street from the Jewish Agency, the nearest thing to a Jewish government in Jerusalem. The Stern Gang was fighting the British, trying to get them to leave Palestine.

1. Kramer, *A History of Palestine*, 143–7.
2. Kramer, *A History of Palestine*, 147–8.
3. Kramer, *A History of Palestine*, 148–51.

The afternoon of March 1st, I was in our room and Sharon was holding on to the bars of the little balcony, which faced the Goldsmith Club. We heard machine gun fire. I looked out just in time to see the Club swelling up like a balloon. I yelled, "Sharon, come in!" As usual, she disobeyed me. Just then, the sound waves hit us. She ran to me, wetting her pants, and threw her arms around me, drenching me. The front of the building separated from the rest and just crumpled. Someone had driven a big truck right up to the door of the building and jumped out before the bomb exploded.

The Club is about 300 yards from our boarding house, with no buildings between. So we spent the afternoon watching the army go into action, putting out the fire, bringing men out of the building on stretchers, and bringing three or four down on ladders from the roof. We had seen those men on the roof when the machine guns were firing and before the explosion. They were noticeable, because they had on shorts and were taking a sunbath. They seemed to be dazed by the concussion and jarring of their building at first; but after a long wait for the ladders, they were able to come down under their own power.

The building was just inside of Security Zone B and our home is just outside of the Zone, but I think we are actually in a safer place than the Club was in. The soldiers told us that men were killed and others are still being uncovered and dug out. This is the first time the terrorists have killed anyone on the Sabbath Day. The strain must be telling on them morally—going around killing people on the Sabbath Day, when there are six other good days for such.

For two weeks, these British soldiers and foreigners had to stay inside a tremendous area. The whole Lancashire Regiment was nearby inside the barbed wire. We missionaries took turns preaching every night to these fellows.

At some point, since we didn't have clerical collars, we missionary men started wearing our white shirts backwards. That way people would know that we were neither Jews nor Muslims and, hopefully, wouldn't shoot us—a real compliment to Christian missions.

The British declared martial law, then lifted it the latter part of April. That spring, the United Nations Special Committee on Palestine met in Jerusalem to discuss the Palestinian crisis. Merrel records, "In the big auditorium of the YMCA, I attended the International Court, with judges from all these different countries debating whether Palestine should be partitioned, divided, or what." In the years to come, Merrel often repeated, "Yesterday's terrorists became today's statesmen." Those words would ring true of both Jewish and Palestinian leaders.

After eight months in the boarding house, the Callaways moved to roomier quarters on the Street of the Prophets. But tragedy followed them:

> The Department of Labor building was blown up a block away from us. The concussion pushed Merrel forward six inches in his chair. Three police were killed and the body of one blown over a fifteen-foot wall. An arm was found three blocks away. Considerable damage was done to the Mission House of the Christian and Missionary Alliance next door to it. The four missionaries there had to spend the night with us, as their rooms were such a mess.
>
> Two nights later, there was a machine gun attack with sporadic rifle shooting in front of our house. Little Sharon was terribly frightened, as was David Lindsey. They kept saying over and over, "The shootings come to get me; the sirens are going to get me."

Beth and Merrel found encouragement with a visit to the church folk in Beirut:

> Old Mr. Jureidini seems to be in a better state of health than when we first came here. Sharon and he had a lovely time together. He loves children and misses being able to see his own grandchildren, who are in America. Sharon calls him "*Juddi Cassees*," or "Grandpa Preacher."
>
> Elias Saleeby does the preaching on Sunday mornings. He truly loves the Lord and is an excellent Bible teacher. The church continues to hold three and four Bible studies each week in the homes of its various members. Recently, a whole family—father, mother, and several children—were baptized into the church.
>
> At one evening service, the national worker, Saleem Sharouk, gave a real missionary sermon, pleading for prayer for other countries and for some of the young folks to give themselves as missionaries. And we have asked the Beirut church to consider us their personal representatives to Arabia, backing us up in prayer.

Over the months of intense language study, Julia Hagood and Finlay Graham realized that God had led them to each other. Bob Lindsey performed their wedding. Merrel spoke as master of ceremonies at the reception. In a nod to the groom's Scottish thrift, Merrel pretended sincerity: "I could understand Finlay's offer to furnish used tea bags from a missionary barrel (instead of champagne). But hanging them out to dry afterwards for the honeymoon trip?" Merrel continued, "Incidentally, Finlay, when Bob indicated that you could kiss the bride, he didn't mean to act like a shot-down RAF [Royal Air Force] pilot in the desert, who's finally found water in the oasis!"

Baptists in the region anticipated another Bible conference for all Baptist missionaries, national workers, and constituency. Pastor Nadeem Boushy in Kefr Mishky would host it. All the planning was left in the hands of the nationals. Merrel and Beth stated, "We believe this is the biblical way of doing things—seeking to develop an indigenous, self-supporting, and self-governing church."

A rattletrap bus replaced donkeys to this conference in the shadow of Mount Hermon, as Beth told it:

> Recently, a rough gravel road has been built and a small native bus goes between Beirut and Kefr Mishky. In true Arab style, the bus called for us two hours late and we all piled in. And I do mean "piled." It was an old, dilapidated nine-seater, windowless and doorless, and we had eighteen in our party, plus two children and luggage for all of us. But the Arab motto is, "There's always room for more." Then halfway up the mountain the driver stopped to take on eight more people. This, however, proved virtually impossible, so a couple of them hung onto the back of the bus and the rest had to be left behind. The trip, which would take about an hour and a half or two hours by car, took us four and a half hours, as the driver had to stop and chat along the way whenever he saw anyone.
>
> But we all arrived in Kefr Mishky tired, but happy, and received a most warm welcome from the Boushy family. Also, the whole village (containing about 1,000 people) was out to watch our arrival. This little village is so high up and isolated that a bus-load of Americans arriving was a real "event" to them.
>
> Because of its altitude, the air is marvelous there and both children thrived. Sharon particularly enjoyed playing with the Arab children. She made herself right at home in the village and everyone loved her. Susan, who is only fifteen months, was a bit overwhelmed by so many strange people. It pleased the people tremendously that we were willing to bring them. Traveling with two small children is not easy anywhere and even more difficult in a purely primitive village with no electricity, running water, sanitary facilities, etc. But the Lord took care of them.
>
> All the meetings there were in Arabic, of course, with national pastors presiding. Each morning we had devotions and inspirational meetings for the Christians. In the afternoon we

had business meetings. Along with other Baptists in Palestine and Lebanon/Syria, we organized ourselves into a Near East Baptist Convention. Then the evenings were given over to purely evangelistic meetings. The little church was packed each night with the village people. We rejoice that five came forward, saying that they wanted to accept Christ as their Savior.

There were a number of problems confronting us as a group and it was wonderful to be able to meet together and really pray about them. It knitted us all together in a greater bond of love and fellowship.

Few seem to have any idea of tithing or giving of their money to the Lord. One of the pastors said, "I can't afford to give to the Lord. I'm too poor." If the pastors have this attitude, it is, of course, no wonder that the people do not give readily to the Lord and his work. The church members in Beirut are learning this lesson and are beginning to give to the Lord.

In the fall of 1947, T.W. Callaway quoted Beth's father in another CCC epistle:

Mr. Fountain: "It looks like the youngsters will be getting into Arabia. I talked yesterday with the electrical engineer of the California Texas Oil Company, just returned from Bahrain. He said, 'Brother, I'll tell you, they are really going out—it's a wild place!' He further said, 'If they have the spirit to go out, don't dampen their spirits; but they'll have one rough time!' I allowed as how they did have the Spirit with a big 'S.'"

Beth sent out a request to prayer partners. "Remember a young Arab girl, Vangy, who has helped in the care of our house and children while we were in school and working. She recently made a real decision for Christ in spite of hinderances from relatives. We hope she might continue to grow spiritually and intellectually."

The United Nations voted on November 29, 1947, on whether or not Palestine should be partitioned into a Jewish state and an Arab state.[4] The Near East clocked seven hours ahead of New York, so Arabs and Jews alike waited anxiously for news of the vote. Finally, word came just before 1:30 a.m. Middle Eastern time. The vote for partition had passed. The Jews wildly celebrated in the streets, locking arm in arm as they sang and danced the *hora* through the night!

---

4. Kramer, *A History of Palestine*, 306.

But by rejecting the Prince of Peace, much darker days would explode in the birthplace of Ishmael and Isaac. Down through the decades, Merrel would often quote Micah 4:3, "They shall beat their swords into plowshares and their spears into pruninghooks: nation shall not lift up a sword against nation, neither shall they learn war anymore."

Prior to leaving Jerusalem for Bahrain, Beth dropped a line to her parents. On at least one occasion, she gathered Susan and Sharon under the bed to protect them from bullets and bombs as she wrote:

> Things here are really getting bad now; it makes one hurt to see all the bloodshed and sorrow . . . The native people are really suffering.
>
> Vangy's family (Arab) who lived in a Jewish section, got two hours' notice from the Haganah [a Zionist military organization] to move. All day long one sees truckloads of household goods of people evacuating to other parts of the city.
>
> Our Jewish newspaper boy was shot and killed the other day. The paper didn't come on schedule and later we learned why.
>
> One Tuesday night, a fine Hebrew Christian boy came into our service. The next day he was beaten and shot in the head in the Old City. He was in a critical condition and taken to the Military Hospital (he works for the Army). There a band of Jews attacked him, because he's a Christian and won't participate in their bloodshed. So now the Army has transferred him to a secret place. When they brought him into the hospital, his only words were, "Gee, Major, I'm sorry to cause you so much trouble."
>
> Merrel was in Zion Square when a Jewish bus came driving pell-mell. He sensed something wrong and followed it to the Emergency Station. There was one dead passenger, several wounded. It had been shot on its way from Hadassah. It has to go through an Arab section. Now they have armored buses . . . It's the borderline places that are dangerous. As *Time* magazine said—There is already partition here and a very real one and woe to the Jew or Arab who oversteps his borders.

An armored car transported the four Callaways in a convoy to the Lydda Airport. A plane took them to Cairo. Due to the unrest in Palestine and cholera in Syria, they flew on a flying boat to Bahrain, a cluster of islands in the Persian Gulf.

Israel declared its statehood May 14, 1948. The bullets, bombs, and bulldozing continue there in the twenty-first century. But the Callaway family escaped the heat of war to share God's cooling water of life in the scorching heat of Arabia.

CHAPTER 14

Bahrain

1948

CRADLED in the warmth of the Persian Gulf, Bahrain's many islands lie between Saudi Arabia on the west and Qatar on the southeast. Despite no landing gear, the flying boat brought the Callaways safely to their destination. "These aircraft differ from floatplanes in that their fuselage itself sits in the water rather than being positioned above it on a pontoon. The flying boat takes its name from the fact that its fuselage is really a boat-like hull."[1]

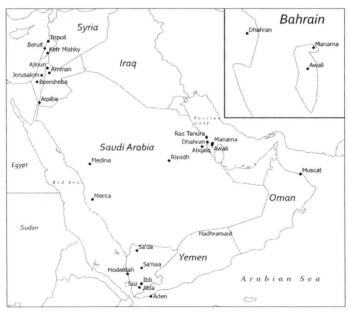

Map of Bahrain and Arabian Peninsula, 1948 (Map courtesy of Steve McCord, Manager of Analysis and Reporting, and Jim Courson, Senior GIS Analyst, International Mission Board, SBC)

1. Yenne, *Seaplanes and Flying Boats*, Introduction, 6.

The family shared the Storms' home until the older couple left on furlough. Ida Storm asked if they had any dirty clothes to send to the *dobi*, the laundry. Beth rejoiced to hear that a laundry existed on the island. A few days later, she rode with a nurse on a deserted stretch of road. The missionary nurse exclaimed, "Oh, there's the *dobi*!" Beth only saw men beating clothes against rocks in a large spring of water.[2] She learned that this rough process left the clothes amazingly clean, despite the sacrifice of shirt buttons.

Other adjustments included the language, the drinking water, and the intense heat. While Bahrainis spoke Arabic, the pronunciation and vocabulary differed from that in Palestine and Lebanon. Instead of using the Arabic greeting for "How are you?" they asked, "What is your color today?"

Water, water everywhere, but not a drop they wanted to drink. Between its high mineral content and the microscopic swarms of bacteria, the water's salt water taste failed to quench one's thirst.

The torrid summer temperatures yielded in fall and spring to bearably warm weather. Winters remained pleasant, except for the dampness. "The rugs feel wet in the mornings," Beth wrote, "and even stockings don't dry overnight."

Local housing varied. In the city, wealthier homes displayed arches to catch the prevailing breeze. White stone walls surrounded outside and inner courts. There people kept all their possessions, wives, children, and animals. Because of the intense heat, in summer most people slept on their roofs, as did the missionaries.

Outside the city proper, poorer residents lived in huts made of date-palm sticks. The homes consisted of many huts built around a small court-yard—one hut for the living room, others for the bedroom and the kitchen. Some structures appeared crude. Beth pointed out, though, "It is amazing to see how they can be fixed up with a little thought and neatness!"

Almost 100 percent of Bahrainis followed Islam. *Muezzins* intoned the call to prayer five times daily from the slender minarets. Single wayside buildings welcomed travelers in transit at prayer time.

---

2. This author obtained most of the information in Chapter 14 from Merrel, Beth, and T.W. Callaway's family letters. However, much of these experiences are also recounted in a Southern Baptist publication: Beth Callaway, "Epistles from Today's Apostles: Missionary Mother in Pioneer Field," in *The Commission*, 1,22; and Merrel P. Callaway, "We Pioneer for Kingdoms," in *The Commission*, 6-7, 32.

Merrel and Beth Callaway with Bahraini man and boy, ca. 1948.
(Photo courtesy of the International Mission Board, SBC)

Arab women wore multiple layers of clothing in public. Aside from toenails peeking out, they resembled black clouds billowing down the street.

During their two and a half years on the island, Merrel worked at the American Mission Hospital, helping in the pharmacy. He told of a religious healer from Yemen. The way this guy healed was to write something from the Qur'an on a piece of paper, give it to a person, and say, "Now, you dissolve this in water and then drink it."

Merrell wrote:

A patient came to the counter at our pharmacy for medicine and I said, "Where's your prescription, your paper?"

"Oh, I ate it," he replied.

Each morning at eight o'clock, Beth joined morning prayer time at the Women's Hospital. The national staff came, along with the two Indian nurses and the sweepers and cleaners. All but the nurses wore their Muslim veils to the service. At 9:30, another service began for the clinic patients.

Merrel attended similar devotional times in the Men's Hospital. He and Mr. Luidens talked with clinic patients and gave out Scripture.

Beth thrilled to teach the Bible to schoolgirls. She believed, "Prayer and only prayer can make these girls take the all-important step of accepting Christ and acknowledging him publicly."

Merrel recalls an encounter with an enforcer:

> Once a week in Bahrain, I went to a small thatch-roof building. I told Bible stories to men who had come to the mission hospital originally, because they had been pearl divers in the Persian Gulf. This was before they had underwater breathing apparatuses. It was so hard on their lungs that they all had the same trouble.
>
> Along with them came a *matauwa*, a religious policeman. (If a girl isn't dressed with a veil, they punish her. Basically, they maintain the morals of the community.) One day, he stayed on after the others left and said, "*Cassees*, (pastor), you know, if you would just say in earnest, 'There is no other God but Allah,' I can promise that in paradise someday you'll have fifty beautiful young maidens at your beck and call."
>
> I said, "*Matauwa*, is that fair to the one I've already got? To Beth?"
>
> He said not to worry about that. "God will give you the strength to do right by all of them."

Arabs, Indians, Britishers, and Americans, to name a few, populated Manama, the capital on the northeastern corner of the main island. The town of Awali sat in the center of Bahrain. Merrel taught the New Testament book of Romans to about fifty Indian young men there. "Some of them come from a church (the Syrian Church of Malabar) that claims to have been established by St. Thomas, the apostle, and is therefore neither Roman Catholic nor Protestant. Thomas is supposed to have made a trip to India."

"Arabs are famed for their hospitality," Beth enthused. "Succulent roasted mutton perched atop mounds of rice and fragrant spices is a feast for the eyes, nose, and palate! Speaking of eyes, the guest of honor at such a banquet is blessed with the sheep's eye. It would be rude to reject such a delicacy. Merrel made sure he was never the most honored guest."

The oil company asked Merrel to fly to the Arabian Peninsula once a month to "lecture" on Sunday mornings to the American oilmen. He said, "I was on a trip to minister in Saudi Arabia that included officiating at the funeral of the wife of an Aramco official. On hearing that my wife was in Bahrain expecting a baby, an Aramco official insisted that the whole family enjoy a half-filled plane going to Lebanon." He told Merrel that no baby should have to be born in the excruciating heat of Bahrain. Merrel recalls sitting on a porch outside Tripoli, Lebanon. He felt the texture of his skin change as it soaked in the cool, moist mountain air. Joy was born at Kennedy Memorial Hospital.

Four days before the family's first Christmas in Bahrain, a cold spell began with lots of rain. The water made a sea of mud everywhere, with no grass or paved streets. Beth moaned, "Oh, how our house did leak! To go up and down the stairs one really needed rubbers and an umbrella!"

She detailed snippets of their busy holiday:

> I spent Christmas alone with the children, as Merrel had gone by the morning launch over to Saudi Arabia to hold Christmas services for the oil company people there in Dharan, Ras Tanur, and Abaiq. Our electricity took that auspicious occasion to go on the blink (which it frequently does), so we spent the evening and night in the dark.
>
> It is the custom here for the Arabs to come and call on the missionaries throughout Christmas Day. By 8:00 a.m., they had started to come and continued steadily all morning. No sooner did one person or group leave than more came. I almost felt like I was a three-ring circus, trying to greet all the guests and carry out the needs of the three children.
>
> Many of those who came to call came out of genuine respect and desire to make acknowledgement of our day of rejoicing. One could not help but appreciate their thoughtfulness. Others, however, many of whom we had never seen before, came hoping that we would be in an expansive mood and give gifts and money. . . . One woman even started to disrobe to show me her "operation" in order to elicit sympathy in the form of money.

Merrel arrived home at 11:55 a.m., dead tired from his busy time of travel and services. But the day was just beginning. At the girls' and women's parties, Beth told the Christmas story using a flannelgraph.

When the Storms returned to Bahrain and the Harrisons left on furlough, the Callaways switched houses. "Other missionaries commented on how tastefully and beautifully Beth decorated the humblest missionary houses," Merrel revealed.

The missionaries appreciated invitations to local homes. Ida Storm's ability to share the gospel in attractive and unexpected ways impressed Beth. "We'll be discussing something far from religion and, all of a sudden, there will be a Testament in her hand and she will be saying, 'That reminds me of something Jesus said.'"

Two recent converts especially touched Beth's heart:

> Fatima is a lovely lady of the upper class, refined and intelligent. Her salvation is the result of many years' labor and prayers. She is

one of the few who can read—not even the leading wife of the head Sheik can read. She is taking a fearless stand for Christ and witnessing earnestly to her Muslim friends and relatives. She wants to be baptized soon, but has not quite gotten up the courage to take that step. She has already been threatened by her family that, if she is baptized, which will definitely commit her to Christianity, they will report her to the Muslim authorities and see that she suffers for it. She just calmly says, "I am of age. I can do what I want. I have found the Light and the Truth and I intend to follow it."

By way of contrast, I should mention Meena. She is a recent convert, baptized last Easter. She is an old, withered-up, mostly blind lady, black as midnight. She is a most lovable person and really loves the Lord. She, too, had been hearing the gospel for many years before she accepted it.

But it is a joy to see these two in the women's meetings. They are so different, yet a stranger entering the room could easily point these two out as somehow similar to one another and different from the others. They are the two that know the Lord and it shows in their faces, obvious joy in hearing the message, and their whole manner of bearing, in contrast with the others. It is a wonderful testimony of what the Lord can do—for rich and poor alike. "Ye are all one in Christ Jesus" [Galatians 3:28] seems particularly applicable here.

Merrel wrote a magazine article that appealed for Southern Baptist doctors to help open doors for work between Aden and Oman in Southern Arabia.

"Lorne Brown," Merrel explained, "was finishing his residency at the University of Tennessee Medical School and also attended the Baptist Young People's Union at church. Someone showed my article to Lorne and he said, 'Why, I went to college with that boy! He took the article home to Gin (wife Virginia).'" Virginia and Lorne did apply as missionaries to Arabia with the Southern Baptist Foreign Mission Board. The Board accepted them. The family made plans to move to Bahrain in the fall.

Meanwhile, some missionary women enjoyed island wedding hospitality. Drumming signaled the start of festivities, which lasted for several days. Beth recorded their experience:

The son of the ruling Sheikh has just married and last week we were invited to "view the bride." First, we went to the palace, where the Queen received us and gave us refreshments for about an hour.

Then she took us to see the bride in her new bridal chamber. The Queen is a very nice woman and I respect her very much.

The men's entrance is quite impressive and it is this what is seen from the road. But the women's is another matter, as is the queen's *majlis*. As we entered the women's unimpressive entrance on the side, I was nearly knocked over by three of the biggest black sheep I've ever seen. Inside the huge courtyard, the place was over-run with sheep, goats, horses, donkeys, cows, and dirty-looking servants' children. Then we were conducted to the room that the queen is given to receive her guests. It was large, but dirty, with no furnishings at all, save three mangy-looking rugs (just small rugs covering about a sixth of the room). By contrast, the Sheikh's *majlis* is completely covered with fine rugs, fully furnished with chairs, tables, etc. His wives and women guests are not allowed here.

As a matter of fact, the wives are not allowed in the other part of the palace at all, except by special request of the Sheikh. I was very much reminded of Queen Esther and King Ahasuerus. That story always seemed a bit far-fetched to me, but not anymore. Now I have actually seen it as it must have been. I can well imagine Esther's trepidation at approaching her husband.

That year, Beth's mother, Florence, poignantly expressed, "It is over four years since we have seen Beth and I do get times when it seems I just must see her. But never once have I wished that she hadn't become a missionary, for she is on the 'King's business.'"

Summer arrived, bringing the usual blast of heat. The family took a ship to India to vacation in cooler climes. "Mind-boggling" sums up their trip from Bahrain's shore to their larger vessel:

We were told to be at the pier at 6:00 a.m. (Ships anchor three miles out and we are taken out in a launch.) But we waited till 8:30 and still no word from the ship. There had been a sandstorm and they couldn't see and there was a high north wind with a frightful sea, so we went back home till 3:00. They couldn't take us out in the regular launch, as the waves were too high.

So, we went in a large, crude Arab sailing *dhow* pulled by a tug and we sat on our luggage. My how we did roll and pitch! Sharon vomited (in spite of the pills) and got quite scared when she was sure we were all going to land in the sea. I stood it fine. But the real fun came getting on the ship.

The problem was how to make the transfer, as the sea was so boisterous. Going up the gang ladder was out of the question. For half an hour we couldn't get near enough to the ship for fear our boat would be dashed to pieces against the larger one.

Finally, we got in position next to a door on the lowest deck. When we were in the trough of a wave, we were way below the door. But when on the crest, we were level with it. So, we all had to make a flying leap (one by one, of course) from our boat to the arms of waiting officers as the boat reached the crest of a wave. The children were *thrown*—the only possible way to get them there. So, it was quite an experience and one I don't want to repeat. Sharon and Mrs. Luiden screamed bloody murder and some oil company folks kept saying, "Take us back to Bahrain; don't let us die!"

Dr. Yerkes's son-in-law, whom Merrel had met on the military transport in 1945, asked Merrel to speak at the Biblical Seminary of Yoknow in the Berar Province of India, north of Bombay (renamed Mumbai). The family vacationed in cooler sections of India. On one train trip, a monkey reached in the window and stole three-year-old Susan's cookie out of her hand.

Dr. Lorne and Virginia Brown arrive in Bahrain with daughters Martha and Pinkie. Merrel Callaway helps unload their luggage from the woodie station wagon, Fall 1949. (Photo courtesy of the International Mission Board, SBC)

The Callaways returned home in plenty of time to give the Browns, with their daughters Martha and Pinkie, a rousing welcome. That fall, the two families rented the first house paid for by Baptists. The Callaways lived upstairs, the Browns downstairs.

Merrel clarified, "We were truly there at the courtesy of the American Mission of the Reformed Church of America. But we Baptists did contribute to medical work by Lorne Brown and by the evangelistic and pastoral work that I was able to do there in Bahrain and Saudi Arabia. There were many months when I was the only ordained Protestant minister there. And at that time, Beth was the only one who could play the big pump organ at church."

For some time, Beth and Merrel had been burdened for Vangy, the Arab girl who had cared for Sharon and Susan in Jerusalem. Vangy had written them frequently, asking to come and look after their daughters on the island. Because of the responsibility to ask a young girl to come there, they hesitated. But, finally, God led them and the Browns to ask her if she would be willing to take nurse's training. She could then work as a nurse in their proposed hospital in South Arabia. They felt that this would allow Vangy to have an active part in spreading the gospel of Christ.

The Southern Baptist Foreign Mission Board also planned to send out the McRaes, a doctor and wife team, and Ruth Swan, a nurse, for the new ministry in Yemen.

Merrel's uncle Timothy Fulton Callaway, better known as Uncle Snap, was a pastor and had twice been elected president of the Georgia Baptist Convention. He wrote his brother Timothy Walton about Beth and Merrel. "I am surely thankful that reinforcements are arriving over there to help them. I don't know anybody in the world, to my way of thinking, who is paying a greater price of love, loyalty, and sacrifice than those two kids over there. When I think of them, I feel that I have never touched the Hem of the Garment when it comes to real consecration."

But the Callaways' and the Browns' vision for "neglected Arabia" did not come to fruition at that time. They were bitterly disappointed and frustrated that Yemen, the Hadramaut, and Saudi Arabia remained closed to the gospel. Merrel tells the tale:

> Lest one sounds occupied with what *we* were doing in Bahrain, let me illustrate what *God* was doing: Beth and I at 11:30 at night were asked to come to another missionary's house for a very important meeting. The whole Arabian Mission was agonizing over the fact that a Muslim fellow might kill his sister. The girl had married a blind man who'd learned to weave baskets and to read in braille and had become an outstanding Christian. She confessed Christ also. He died, leaving her with a small child and a good name.

However, she was weak spiritually and not as strong mentally. She was seduced by an Indian man who worked nearby and she was expecting a baby out of wedlock. If her pregnancy became known, her strongly Muslim brother, who was already enraged at her becoming a Christian, would likely kill her for the added disgrace to the family. Thus, until late in the night, we and all the missionaries discussed how to get this pregnant woman and her two-year-old child out to a place where she could have her delivery in safety.

Long after midnight someone suggested that the widow and small child should be sent to a Christian hospital, where she could deliver her baby and hopefully be influenced for Christ in a real way. On being asked if I knew of such a hospital between Bahrain and the Mediterranean, I mentioned my friend Dr. Hargreaves at the Church Mission Society Hospital, Gaza, and Dr. Charles McLean of the hospital in Ajloun, Jordan. I knew Dr. McLean only because Finlay Graham had told me of his need. His letter of thanks had sealed our friendship.

It was decided to send cablegrams to both men making the same request. I don't think that Dr. Hargreaves ever received his message. But McLean said, "Bring her on up." The missionaries decided (when I was obviously weak from lack of sleep) that I should fly with the widow and child to see them safely in Dr. McLean's care in Ajloun.

As she and I were in the plane over the Gulf, she'd think the air pocket meant we'd end up in the water. She'd reach across the aisle and grip my arm in a vice. She thought I could keep her from falling. In Bosrah, I got out to show our passports. Hers had no photo; it just said, "*Purdah*," or "behind the veil." I could tell they wondered what this American man was doing taking a Muslim woman across a border. In those days, the passports said . . . "missionary." I pointed to that word and it's a wonderful tribute to Christian missions that they let me through. The same thing happened in Iraq, Syria, and Jordan.

By the time we got to Ajloun and I was standing in front of Dr. McLean's hospital, I didn't know how I felt after all I'd been through. That was the first time I had seen Dr. McLean or the hospital. But when a British lady nurse walked up to me and welcomed me with "Praise the Lord," it did something to me. All I know is, I felt at home. I knew everything was okay. That changed everything!

Merrel left the expectant widow and her young child in the care of the McLeans and returned to his own family on Bahrain. But that would not be the last he would see of Ajloun.

On VE Day (Victory in Europe) in 1945, Merrel, Beth, and Sharon had sailed for Palestine on a military transport vessel. Five years later, they boarded a ship in Alexandria for the United States of America. This time, though, they stowed away "extra baggage"—Susan and Joy. Excitement ran rampant. But their time home with family would be cut short.

CHAPTER 15

Whither Goest Thou?

1950

T HE family of five safely surged across the Atlantic. They reunited with the Fountains in New Jersey and extended family at James Island, South Carolina, before renting a house in Bloomfield, New Jersey, near Chatham.

Six-year-old Sharon developed osteomyelitis, a serious infection of the bone. Doctors removed dead bone tissue in her right shin bone (tibia). She required several courses of antibiotics. Her parents updated the CCC:

> Merrel: We have been sorry that we could not join in the reunion on the island in recent days. While waiting on the Lord's will, I would like to do some evangelistic meetings, missionary rallies, and expository preaching in this country.

> Beth: Just a hasty note as we have returned from the hospital with Sharon. There is still infection in Sharon's leg and the wound is still open. She has to wear a new cast until September, then more x-rays; and then we will see what further treatment is necessary. This is a bitter blow to us all, of course, for we had hoped she was all well. The cast is so hot and awkward. Even after it is off, she will have to use crutches for a while.

A Chatham newspaper interviewed the couple. Merrel told the staff correspondent, "The Muslim believes that God is great. By our help, we're showing them that God is love, too."

Back in the Middle East, Gilead Memorial Hospital in Jordan contin- ued to drain Dr. and Mrs. McLean's meager finances. They hoped to open a small clinic in a nearby town and do some evangelistic work before they retired to England. They offered their hospital in Ajloun free of charge to the Southern Baptist Foreign Mission Board.

Dr. Sadler visited the Reformed missionaries in Arabia with whom the Browns and Callaways had worked. After discussions, he concluded that it was time for Baptists to establish their own work elsewhere and not be an appendage of the Reformed Mission. In his letter to Merrel of April 25, 1950, he insisted:

> You understand, of course, that I am not a quitter. At the same time, I do not believe we would be well-advised to keep a size-able group of missionaries in [Bahrain and nearby areas] without a definite project in mind. This is especially true since there are other places whose needs cry out for the services these missionaries can render. . . .
>
> Let me say again, I appreciate the manner in which you and Beth and the Browns have fitted into the situation there. It is evident that the Reformed Church missionaries appreciate the service you have rendered.

Meanwhile, the Callaways and Browns passionately wished to develop medical work and evangelistic outreach in Arabia. The McRaes and Miss Swan waited for word in the States, having planned to go to Bahrain. Now all that was off.

Airmail letters flew furiously among the Callaways, Miss Swan, and the McRaes in America; Dr. Sadler in Zurich, Switzerland or England; the Browns in Bahrain or Oman doing medical work or in Lebanon for language study; and the McLeans in Ajloun, to name just a few of those involved. One such letter reached Merrel and Beth on July 5, 1950, from Lorne Brown. He told of his visit to the McLeans as requested by Dr. Sadler:

> I went there rather expecting the place to be quite adequately supplied with mission work, but instead the need is really very great. This is the only mission hospital in the entire country and it is in the center of the most populous district. Two-thirds of the population of Trans-Jordan live in 176 villages scattered over *Jebel* [Mountain] Ajloun. There is only one other surgeon in the entire country—an Italian in Amman. Of course, there are not vast stretches of unoccupied territory that there is in Arabia; but there is a fairly dense population untouched by Christian missions, except Catholic, and certainly plenty to keep us busy for a lifetime.
>
> Gin and I feel that we would be very happy there and that we would be doing as much to spread the gospel as we would in

Arabia. . . . Perhaps you think that we are willing to switch our
affections from Arabia on very short notice; but we can't help
believing that from the human standpoint at least, this is a most
wonderful opportunity. We will be anxious to have your reaction
to the situation.

Merrel responded:

Dear Lorne and Gin,

The wonderful way in which the Lord has led the [Finlay]
Grahams and Callaways into fellowship with and respect for the
McLeans is an indication to me that he is evidently in this proposi-
tion . . . and I believe that the McLeans' offer and our hoped-for
Southern Baptist acceptance is the Lord's doing.

However, Beth and I would like to see Southern Baptists, in
their forward advance, attempt both the Trans-Jordan and Arabia
projects. Southern Baptists, if faced with the challenge, have the
resources to do both jobs. I'm not even facing any distant possibilities, such as the awful possibility of the Browns eventually landing
at Ajloun and the Callaways in Arabia. As terrible as that seems to
us, we can leave that in the Lord's hands for future guidance.

Dr. McLean informed the Callaways in July 1950 about the pregnant
widow Merrel had brought to the hospital. "She was delivered last week of a
baby boy. [The mother] had been not frightfully well and Dr. Dorey was not
at all sure that she would get a living baby. However, the youngster is very
well and our immediate problem is to get him housed. I see [the mother's]
"*laissez passer*" [a permit] expires on August 22, so it would be well to get
her back to Bahrain before that time."

He added that they were willing to have Vangy work at the hospital as
a probationer. McLean's October 31 missive stated, "Vangy has been with
us for over a fortnight. We are very pleased at the way Vangy is settling in.
Sister [the head nurse] is excellent at initiating and she made Vangy feel she
was wanted and could help."

Cornelia Dalenberg, a missionary nurse in Bahrain, let the Callaways
know in her September letter that the widow's newborn was being adopted
by a Canadian missionary in Bethlehem, Palestine.

The Southern Baptist Foreign Mission Board officially accepted the
McLeans' offer of the Ajloun hospital in September. They poured in funds
to secure much-needed running water, electricity, fly screening, as well as
an x-ray machine, a laboratory, and refrigeration. While the hospital was
free, it was not cheap. Other requirements included missionary housing,

a men's dormitory, a nurses' house, a power house, and for exercise and recreation a tennis court. The big question: Who would staff it?

In mid-December, Pat Storm and Lorne Brown made an exploratory trip to Aden and across the Hadramaut in Southern Arabia to assess the probability of Baptists being able to start mission work in those areas. They covered much territory and talked with several officials in Aden and the Hadramaut. They found that the prospect of bringing in a medical team was slim and any evangelistic thrust nil.

Dr. Brown reported to Dr. Sadler on December 27, "We are greatly saddened that Southern Arabia still remains closed; but on the other hand, I am impressed with the great opportunities for missions *now* in Jordan. If we can establish a strong base in Jordan, in later years it will be much easier to open in Southern Arabia."

Lorne added a personal note to Merrel and Beth to his official report. "I know that you will be sad at hearing of these closed doors. I have asked Sadler to transfer us [Browns] to Ajloun. It is my own conviction that there is little more that can be done in Bahrain. Hope you are well now, Merrel. With love, Lorne."

George Sadler wrote the Callaways in January of 1951, confirming that "the door to Arabia is closed to Southern Baptists for the time being at least. That means, of course, that you will have to rethink your plans. Praying for you God's guidance."

Virginia and Lorne Brown, with Pinkie and Martha, made plans to move shortly to Ajloun. Ruth Swan and the McRaes, with their boys, would join them after language study in Beirut.

In his letter of January 28 to Beth and Merrel, Lorne shared, "From my two visits to Ajloun, we think that there is a tremendous opportunity for evangelism as well as for medicine. If there is one need of the mission there that seems greater than any other, it is for a pastor. McLeans and their assistants have done a great job, but they just need a pastor and we can't think of anyone that would be better than the Callaways."

That new year, Merrel reminded Drs. Rankin and Sadler that he had told them that he wished to take a course at Columbia during his furlough. George Sadler wrote him on January 28, "However, the Board is not prepared to finance such a study unless it is designed to fit the missionary for some special task to which he will address himself on his return to the field."

The Callaways, of course, had not yet made a firm decision as to their next field of service, but the new mission work in Jordan was their most likely destination. Merrel clarified his reasons for wanting advanced study:

> I want to study in the field of Islamics and Arabic Literature. Such courses as Islamic Civilization are of importance in dealing with Muslims about their souls. Knowing their background helps. Perhaps these studies might not sound "designed to fit the missionary for some special task"; but when one remembers that the McRaes, Browns, and Miss Swan have had practically no studies in Islamics, it would seem as though the evangelist, at least, should try to be better acquainted with the literature, religious, political, and social institutions of Islam and the Islamic contribution to civilization, particularly in the fields of science and philosophy.
>
> I feel that the courses mentioned will fit me better for anything that develops in the future.

The Board approved his request for funding. "From Long Hill," Merrel said, "Beth and I would drive in one day a week to NYC in which Dr. Jeffry taught a course. Consequently, I visited Zwemer. He had said, 'Come down to my apartment and we can have lunch across the street.' Then he took me to his apartment. He said, 'I found this book in a used bookstore. Of the fifty books I've written, this is the best,' and he gave it to me. He told me that as he wrote the book in Bahrain, he had to wear towels on his arms because the perspiration would ruin the ink on the page." The Callaway family treasures this copy of *Arabia: The Cradle of Islam*.[1]

Merrel and Beth recognized God's open door leading them to work in Jordan, the Hashemite Kingdom.

Lorne Brown shared with the Callaways from Ajloun on April 8, "We enjoy seeing Vangy. She is a very fine girl and is making a good nurse. Merrel, I'm about to catch up with you, only my third is going to be a boy."

And Merrel's father compiled another CCC letter:

> As you doubtless know, Merrel, Beth, and the three little girls were to spend the entire month of July with us, but a cablegram from Dr. Sadler called them back to Trans-Jordan after a week's visit with us. We are certainly sorry to see them go.
>
> Merrel: The assassination of King Abdullah of Jordan is another reason for requesting your prayers for us, our field, and our work,

---

1. Zwemer, *Arabia: The Cradle of Islam*.

as we leave Idlewild Airport [now Kennedy], New York, at 7 p.m., July 29th.

Mr. Fountain: The Arabs have really flown. It was pretty tough to see them enter the plane, then take off into the air and out of sight in a few minutes. They caused a lot of comment, as people saw those three little ones go ahead—little Joy carrying her blue bag, swaggering out to the plane as if she had always flown and as if she owned the plane.

Sharon was very quiet all day Sunday and I don't think she wanted to leave, although she did not say so.

The grandparents had given each girl a booklet of paper dolls—cardboard dolls with an assortment of paper outfits to punch out delicately. Those helped the children occupy the tedious twenty-eight flight hours.

As the airplane propelled them eastward toward Jordan, who would know how heavy sat the crown on the new head of the Hashemite Kingdom?

CHAPTER 16

Moonlight over the Mediterranean

1949

T EN thousand miles west of Ajloun, a twenty-seven-year-old nurse from Iowa took stock of her life. Arlene Jensen had graduated from nursing school, worked at hospitals in St. Paul and Harlan, and completed the University of Minnesota programs in Nursing Education and in Public Health. She then taught nursing at her old school.

But what about her youthful commitment to missions?

Arlene contacted the newly formed Baptist General Conference Mission Board. In her spring of 1949 interview with General Secretary of the Board Walford Dan Danielson, he said, "I just had a call for someone with your qualifications to go to Tespur in Assam, India, to prepare to open a nursing school when the hospital is ready." Amazing!

"I had thought a lot about Assam," Arlene admitted. "My missionary heroine was there, but I thought it was too obvious. But this was an open door, so I agreed to test it out. I asked the Lord to stop me if it was not his will."

The Mission Board accepted her for medical service in the province of Assam. She would sail on a freighter from New York with a handful of other missionaries. Her diary and letters home sometimes cast differing perspectives on events. What we write in "Dear Diary" is not always what we write to "Dear Mommy."

While she dearly loved her relatives in Iowa, many family members had little understanding of why she was going to Assam. At the big send-off picnic in Harlan, they made the usual comments---"Wonderful adventure!" "Good luck!" "Will you like it?" "Take care of yourself." While it would be an adventure, her purpose for going was to share Christ and care for people's medical needs.

Arlene boarded a train for St. Paul. She made her home base at Esther Blackmore's house, then went to multiple meetings and other friends' homes. Having lived in St. Paul for most of the past ten years, she recognized that much of her spiritual family dwelt in the Twin Cities. She collected her passport and bought a new footlocker to contain all the gifts showered upon her. Mounds-Midway alumnae threw a farewell fest for her. A church service seemed "almost like a Danish Baptist reunion." And InterVarsity Christian Fellowship gave a hot dog roast in her honor.

She wrote home, "By that time I was having dreams about saying goodbye. I woke up in the middle of the night hugging my pillow and kissing it and saying, 'goodbye.' More fun!"

A Blackhawk pullman car carried Arlene, assorted Mission Board personnel, and two other new missionaries, Dr. Charles (Chuck) and May Merchant with toddlers Danny and Mary. They dealt with business during the stopover in Chicago at Mission Headquarters, then pressed on through the next night on the Broadway Limited to New York City.

Wednesday afternoon, September14, they boarded their ship, the SS *Steel Fabricator*. The ship's cargo included steel for building an oil pipeline in Syria; Lincoln and Ford cars; Caterpillars; and US currency to drop off in Djibouti for Haile Selassie, Emperor of Ethiopia.

left to right **Dr. Charles and May Merchant, Arlene Jensen, and Rev. Walford and Ann Danielson board the SS *Steel Fabricator* for seven-week journey to Assam, India 1949. (Photo courtesy of Converge)**

Walford Danielson and his wife Ann sailed with them. They would survey the various Baptist General Conference of America mission fields. Arlene found her cabin mate, Henrietta Watson, congenial. Henrietta was heading to Bombay for her second missionary term.

Henrietta and Arlene climbed out of their bunks at 2:30 a.m. to watch tugs pull and push the *Fabricator* out from the dock. After a stop in Philadelphia, the ship turned southeast. The two cabin mates thanked God for the privilege of going on mission. They rested in Psalm 4:8: "I will both lay me down in peace, and sleep: for thou, Lord, only makest me dwell in safety." And safe they were. Ten days later, though, the captain told them that the fog had been so heavy that first night that they almost hit a sister ship!

Early in the voyage, the galley prepared rice and curry for supper. "I can't say it's wonderful," Arlene confessed, "but perhaps the Lord can give me a love for even that."

Fierce winds blew across the Atlantic. Arlene tried to type on deck. She folded half of her steamer robe under the machine on her lap and with the other half held down the paper. She wrote: "I just made a dash for the pantry for crackers. Honestly, this ship is just like sitting on a swing—up and down—and leaves one's stomach feeling the same way. You don't let it get empty." One night, rough seas tossed their steward out of his bunk. After dinner the next evening, a giant wave arched over the deck and drenched the Danielsons. Their cabin porthole was open, so salt water soaked their beds too.

Near the Azores, the missionaries held their first Sunday service on deck, joined by several crew members.

Passengers saw their first glimpse of Spain, Gibraltar, and North Africa. Arlene described Tangier:

> The city extended about five miles along the coast. Way up the mountain were beautiful homes and scattered around were huge buildings. On the cape was a lighthouse and farther up a mosque. All the buildings were white with red roofs.
>
> Sparks, our radio operator, was very generous with his field glasses. Did you know that "Sparks" is automatically the name of any radio operator on any ship? This young fellow has another year at Michigan State, but is taking this year out. The radio room and his place are on the same deck as ours, so we see him more than the other officers.

They passed by Gibraltar:

> Someone on the Rock signaled us with Morse code using a light—
> "Who are you?" "Where are you going?" "When do you expect to
> arrive?" Our second mate answered. Sparks told us what he was
> saying. We could see a huge structure on the very top of the Rock,
> probably a powerful short-wave radio station. There were numer-
> ous buildings—a town—at the base of the Rock. As we passed and
> looked back, on this side was a huge watershed—flat concrete—
> covering, it appeared, about one-third of the side of the Rock. It is
> used to collect water.

Sparks began to feature more frequently in Arlene's diary:

> Sept. 29 My heart is full this evening. Sat on deck—lovely music,
> thanks to Sparks. Gorgeous moon making silvery path—lonely, so
> lonely for something I never had; so came in and prayed. Praise
> God's name for Ephesians 3:16, "That he would grant you accord-
> ing to the riches of his glory to be strengthened with might by his
> Spirit in the inner man." Show me many things, Lord, that will
> prepare me to serve thee rightly.

> Sept. 30 All out to see Malta, where [the apostle] Paul was ship-
> wrecked. Came in at 11:30. Sparks invited me to the bridge—risky.
> Won't do it again, because it worried Matties [a crew member] and
> definitely isn't right. Henrietta and I claimed Sparks for the Lord.

In early October, they docked in Beirut, Lebanon. The contrast between lovely hotels and ragged people curled up in doorways of modern
buildings shocked Arlene. She grieved to see barefoot workers bent over
double with huge loads as they wound through narrow hilly streets. Children watched her with pitiful, bloodshot, begging eyes. Some women wore
colorful flowered dresses, others conservative Western dress. Priests of all
types walked the crooked streets. Arlene noted men bowing their heads to
the ground on their rugs at the Muslim prayer time. She even saw two men
praying "on top of the crates which were unloaded from our ship."

At Alexandria, Egypt, workers hauled their vessel by ropes to the dock.
Henrietta, Arlene, Mr. Singh (one of the Indian passengers), and two crew
members, Sparks and Matties, made the 150-mile trip to the pyramids. Arlene chronicled their adventure:

> We went through the Sahara Desert on the way. We saw many evi-
> dences of war—one whole field of old German tanks, many desert-
> ed and wrecked buildings, and ever so much tangled barbed wire,

as well as the location of a former German Army prison camp. As we went on, the area became more barren and sand dunes came in sight.

As soon as we arrived, we were put in charge of an old character in a flowing robe and turban, who with a candle led the way into the largest of the pyramids. The tunnels were so low we had to bend to walk through. We climbed up a stairway-ladder incline to about 225 feet, halfway to the top. Then, we had to bend even lower to go through a short tunnel into the king's tomb. The coffin there was empty, hewed out of one huge piece of stone. At intervals, they would light for us a flare of magnesium, so we could see better.

The architecture is amazing! Huge blocks of stone over six feet long by three feet wide and several feet thick, ranging in weight up to at least six tons. There were only nine of these in the ceiling of the king's tomb and it was too large for a living room. To think that not a speck of mortar was used is really a marvel. Each stone was dovetailed together—most remarkable. Then, we went way down to the queen's tomb directly under the king's. We bumped our heads several times.

We didn't get to see much of Alexandria. There are two huge crates or boxes on our deck and we finally asked the captain what was in them. He said, "Snow plows bound for Bombay." Doesn't that seem odd?

At 11 p.m. that night, the freighter entered the narrow Suez Canal along with about five other ships in their convoy. Once in the Red Sea, deck hands put up awnings on both sides of the deck due to the sun's intense heat. With the prevailing wind behind them and the ship traveling at about the same speed (eighteen knots), the humid, still air smothered. Fans in the cabins made the heat slightly bearable. Someone suggested that the only thing red about the Red Sea was the red-hot temperature. The sea varied from 300 to 600 miles wide in places. Sometimes Arlene and Henrietta slept on cots on the deck to escape the sweltering cabin heat.

A pilot boarded from a small craft to guide them into Djibouti's harbor. "It's fun to watch the signal flags," Arlene enthused:

> A black and yellow one means we want a pilot and a two-color one, usually red and white, means he is aboard. A yellow one means we want the quarantine officials or the customs man or some such important official. The one we all look for with excitement is the company agent who has the mail.

All we had for the port was $175,000.00 for Haile Selassie [who owned a home there]. But it took time to unload, because they had to count the boxes and there were a couple hundred, each weighing about 169 pounds. The stevedores were quite tall, but most of them couldn't weigh over 100 pounds. They did not look well-nourished. Their dress was either shorts or skirts wrapped around and shirts.

As the *Fabricator* entered the Indian Ocean, a host of lavender jellyfish floated in the water, "looking like ladies' spring hats." Flying fish leaped up and out of the sea before submerging.

In Bombay, Henrietta's coworker met her on the dock, which surprised and delighted her. May and Chuck Merchant and Arlene glimpsed the Hindu *Divali* festival and the Hindu New Year. Firecrackers exploded. Small lamps lighted walkways "from house to the street to light the way for the goddess of wealth," they were told.

Arlene found the Crawford Market fascinating:

> When you first enter the main market, about a dozen men and boys almost mob you with baskets and offer to carry your purchases. There were two of the cutest little boys there who followed us around. If they do the smallest favor, they expect a handout and mostly you can't prevent them from doing things. These kids were dying to know what my fold-up umbrella was and how it worked. So, I opened it up and showed them, to their delight. Then I held out my hand and said, "*Baksheesh* [money]?" You should have seen them laugh! It was great fun!

Two days later, they reached Columbo, where they explored a Buddhist temple. "There were many rooms, each with a Buddha in a different position with many disciples and angels, etc. The first one was sitting on a throne, the next one reclining, and they were all huge statues much larger than human size. One was of Buddhist priests telling the story to an Indian hunter. All around were paintings of the life of Buddha. He even had a harem."

The weary explorers returned to the ship. They traveled up the Hooghly River, with green on both banks, because the rainy season had just ended. They passed rice fields, cotton and jute mills, and brick-making yards. Budgebudge was a small reef town, almost a suburb of Calcutta, where they dropped off more cargo. Arlene wrote:

> All our stevedores have done such efficient and systematic jobs of unloading. But here, they fought over every barrel containing

rosin for the oil industries here. For rolling a barrel up the pier, they get six *annas* and there is no system, except for each one to get as many as possible. It was terrible! They fought like dogs for each load of eight that came down. They stood under the load and it was really strange that some were not killed.

By afternoon, we could see the buildings of Calcutta. I have never seen such a dirty place! Smoke was almost as thick as fog and gave the whole place a misty, unreal appearance.

Arlene's voyage on the *Steel Fabricator* was ending. Comments about Sparks resurfaced in her diary:

> Nov. 4 Pulled into Calcutta 6 p.m.—dark—smokey—lights of Calcutta eerie. Sparks and I on flying bridge. Doesn't see how I can be so incorruptible. When will you save him, Lord?

> Nov. 5 Sparks wanted my class ring—didn't think I wanted him to have it. I can't understand how I could have such fellowship with darkness—yet I like him so much.

The missionaries disembarked and stayed in the dormitories of the Lee Memorial Mission until they completed all the customs requirements. Ann Davidson and Arlene shared a room. In the heat of Bombay, the ship's water was always hot. Now, in freezing cold Calcutta, the water from the faucets ran cold. Arlene did not appreciate sleeping under mosquito netting. "It is just like being in a cage!" She penned, "You should have seen us at 6 a.m., sitting cross-legged and facing each other on her bed, drinking tea and eating toast and bananas!"

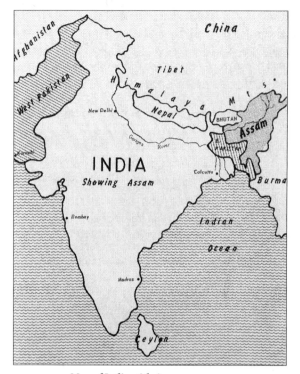

Map of India with Assam, ca. 1949
(Map courtesy of Converge)

The new division of Pakistan from India complicated customs. One first had to clear customs at the dock and then inland customs. Arlene explained the red-tape process. "The stuff had to go through Pakistan to get from Calcutta to Assam. When the steamer goes into Pakistan, it is out of India proper. Then it has to be passed to get back into India again." She added, "You should have seen me running around town in taxis with those huge Sikhs driving. They never cut their hair and wear big turbans around and around their heads. Sometimes we took rickshaws pulled by men."

Cows abounded, as did large cow patties. Arlene wrote to her mother, "Once a whole herd of big, black cows—four or five—were lying right in the middle of the street placidly chewing their cuds. Many times, taxis had to stop and wait for them to get out of the way. In America, the drivers would be swearing, but here they just wait."

While in Calcutta, Sparks and Arlene dined several times at restaurants together:

> Nov. 14 Sparks surely is free about talking. Says I'll be sorry I didn't let him love me. He went home before dinner after much sarcasm. Poor boy. I went home and cried. If he could only know the joy of Christ. Mrs. D. worried about me.

Calcutta had its share of Communists, and riots occurred almost daily, with people being injured and killed. Some burned buses run by the government. Their last day in the city, they witnessed two airplanes collide and drop from the sky. The smoke from the crash rose not too far away.

In India, one could never be sure how long a journey might take. Wise travelers brought their own soap, towels, bedding roll, and food. As Arlene was about to board the train for Harisinga at 10:30 that night, Sparks showed up:

> Nov. 16 Wished he could kiss me goodbye. So did I, but I'm sure it was better not. I'm glad we're parting. I'm getting deeper and deeper myself. Funny how the undesirable qualities fade and the devil makes them in the background. Lord, teach me to recognize temptation and not rationalize.

A hoard of cockroaches greeted Arlene and the Danielsons as they opened the door to their train compartment. Forty minutes later with the help of a flashlight and an insect bomb, they were free for the night.

They awoke to the sight of majestic mountains. Arlene's reaction to the rice and curry? "Ugh!" She prayed to learn to like it. In her letter home, though, she said, "I wish I could tell you how much I love India and how glad I am to be here!"

When their train pulled into Harisinga, Ruth and Warren Johnson, Dorothy Dotz, and Rueben Holms gave them a rousing welcome. Arlene thrilled at the small house she and Dorothy would share for a time. In short order, Arlene was counting out patients' pills in the dispensary connected to their home.

At the evening service, three young girls sang a welcome song and placed leis made of coxcomb, hibiscus, and white flowers around the newcomers' necks. After a welcoming speech by one gentleman, the Danielsons and Arlene gave brief testimonies through a translator. An elderly pastor told them how he had been praying for missionaries to come to the North Bank of the Brahmaputra River. He thrilled to have them finally here.

The next day, Rueben handed Arlene her beginning language books, which she eagerly accepted.

"Tonight, I have to pinch myself to believe I'm in India." She mused, "I wonder how much the ship experience revived my selfishness. I simply cannot stand too much attention. Lord, I need willingness to get up in the a.m. and to discipline for language study and to dig into dirt and germs and to give my all for thee. I'm afraid right now I'm terribly interested in me."

CHAPTER 17

Victory between the Himalayas and the Brahmaputra

1949

Assam is squeezed into the northeastern corner of India. Above it lies the massive Tibetan Plateau and the magnificent Himalayas, with the mountainous country of Bhutan to its northwest. What used to be Burma (now Myanmar) lies to the east and the former East Pakistan (now Bangladesh) bumps its southwest side.

The mighty braidlike Brahmaputra River, known by numerous names, begins its journey in southwestern Tibet (since confiscated by China). The river flows eastward at length before dipping south into India. Forming a giant backward letter C, it curves southwest through Assam, then turns south as it enters present-day Bangladesh. There it unites with the Ganges to sweep finally into the Bay of Bengal.

Arlene focused her work north of the Brahmaputra. She spent much of her time in the towns of Harisinga, Gauhati, and Tezpur. First, though, she arrived at the North Lakhimpur mission station. One nurse friend from Mounds-Midway days, Ethel Hagstrom, was nine months pregnant. Dr. Merchant, Nurse Dorothy Dotz, and Arlene made a great team as they helped Baby Paul Hagstrom into the world.

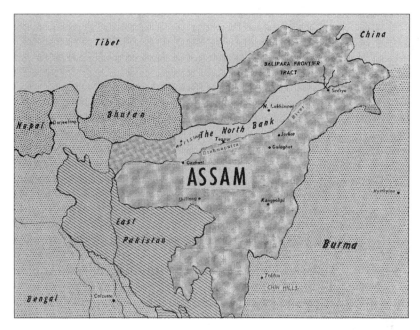

Map of North Bank of Assam, India, ca. 1949
(Map courtesy of Converge)

Worn out from looking after the newborn and the other Hagstrom children as Ethel recovered, Arlene faced the usual culture shock of a new language and new country:

> Dec. 6 Surely haven't had any spiritual food to record. Wonder anew if the Lord can ever use me. It's been too many days now looking for this victory.

> Dec. 7 The Lord has been dealing with me this evening. As usual, the victory over Quiet Time has not been mine. Have been fighting a depression for a couple of days now. I must let the Lord give me grace for victory over this selfishness. Guess Sparks was right when he said I wasn't the type that was sacrificial and really wanted to give up all for India. What he didn't know was that the Lord can supply what I lack. The Lord has been chastening me. Teach me true humility and please, Lord, don't let me have this terrible inferiority complex. Just one more thing, Lord, please save Sparks and then help me forget him. His attentions may be behind this selfishness.

> Dec. 8 Dreamed about Sparks again last night. Told D. I believed if
> he came to the Lord, I could forget him—I wonder . . .

On Christmas Day, she joined other missionaries on a trip to a rural village:

> The roads are really oxcarts and there were rivers. We forded
> six, not small ones either. The new Jeep-truck plowed through the
> water and sand and up the steep banks. What an experience!
>
> The village, Borigau, had invited us, so extensive prepara-
> tions had been made. A huge "Welcome" sign was up and not only
> were we garlanded, but our truck also. The afternoon consisted of
> singing, special numbers, and testimonies from each of us, with a
> message from Dr. Danielson. There were hundreds of people and
> our White Cross pencils, erasers, scissors, and old Christmas cards
> had a hard time going around, even for the children.
>
> After all this, they treated us to the best rice and curry I've
> ever tasted! About 4 p.m., we were glad to start home and get over
> the rivers before dark. How thrilling to visit a village where, of the
> one hundred homes, eighty are Christian!

Holiday over, her studies resumed. "Language study fills the greater part of my time now and I am glad slowly to be getting an understanding of the strange words. I very much appreciate the help of my *pundit* [teacher] Florida Das. I'm trying to translate the fourth chapter of John. Did you know that if one knows all the words in this chapter, you have a very good working vocabulary?"

Dispensary work in Harisinga comprised Arlene's other main job. Her coworker, Dorothy Dotz, was engaged to George Johnson. She would soon fly to the States to be married.

"The week before Dorothy left," Arlene wrote friends, "Meloi Marak arrived, a lovely Garo girl who recently graduated [in nursing] from the Mission Hospital in Gauhati. It isn't easy for a young girl to leave a city and come out to the jungle, so to speak; but she came out and we are praising the Lord daily for her. She not only understands the language, but also the people much better than I possibly could in these few months." Arlene ex-plains, "The ministry of the dispensary is very important, because fully 80 percent of the patients are Hindu or otherwise non-Christian."

While work, study, and adjustment to a new culture occupied much of her time, thoughts of Sparks from the *Fabricator* continued to intrude. She dreamed of him some nights for several months and made a trip to Calcutta in springtime to see him.

On February 16, 1950, her dear friend from St. Paul days, Martha Blackmore, wrote of her concern. "About Sparks, is there something about him you like, or are you both just passing time? Don't let anything injure your testimony or your power with God; you'll regret it all your life."

Mrs. Ann Danielson, one of her shipboard companions and wife of the Mission Executive Director, concurred in her July 9, 1950, letter to Arlene: "I, too, was a bit surprised that you flew to Calcutta to meet Sparks. I realize you must have had a struggle before you came to that decision. If you continue this relationship through mail, I fear it will tend to make you unhappy at heart and no doubt in your work. You may have decided already to make the break."

Arlene mentioned little about the radio operator after this. Perhaps she made the decision to focus on sharing Christ's love and healing power with the people of India.

The mission hoped to build a hospital and start a nursing school in a medically underserved area of Assam. The Board had hired Arlene with this in mind. But first, they had to purchase land and secure government approval. The Mission Field Council agonized over whether such a huge project was feasible. Not only would a hospital have to be built, but housing for the medical staff, support personnel, and nursing students would be needed, not to mention water, electricity, and drainage systems installed.

Years later, Arlene told family members that the foundation for the new hospital replaced the portable landing strip that US forces had used during World War II to "fly over the hump," the Himalayan Mountains, into China. Now, the Air Force Museum in Dayton, Ohio, displays a 3-D model of the region, showing where pilots took off from Assam.[1] These brave airmen brought everything the American forces serving in China needed, since the Japanese had cut off all other routes.

Monsoon rains amazed Arlene. Torrential drops plummeted straight down, turning the ground into a muddy quagmire. She could leave her windows open, though, since the rain didn't blow in.

During her first year in India, she received seven wedding invitations and three birth announcements from close friends and family half a world away.

Arlene updated loved ones about her work:

---

1. This author viewed the model of the region at the Air Force Museum in summer of 1990.

Last Thursday, we started a new venture in the dispensary. Bazaar day is very busy for us. At nine o'clock, before we gave out any medicine, we held a little service. Meloi told those who gathered all about malaria: how it is contracted, treated, and prevented. How attentively they listened! They cannot afford to buy mosquito nets, but others just do not realize their importance. If we can help them stay well, our purpose will be accomplished.

Then Warren Johnson gave them a flannelgraph story on John 4. We've been busy, too, giving all the school children cholera and typhoid shots.

Doctors insisted that nurses know more about running a hospital and how it should be organized than they did. They included Arlene as a vital part of the Hospital Planning Committee. She informed her supporters, "We are busy working on floor plans for the hospital and other buildings in Tezpur."

Tradition decreed that each Easter morning students garbed in white serenaded the missionaries with hymns of Jesus' resurrection before dawn. Arlene thrilled to the message. She never forgot their ministry of blessing and triumph.

She passed her First-Year Assamese Exam on December 15 and 16. Next, she tackled the harder second year. She informed Iowa church friends how thrilling it was "to be able to tell the Christmas story to a group of Hindu women who came over to visit Christmas Day, using a picture book of the life of Christ which some of you made."

Rev. Paul and Dr. Laura Edwards arrived with their children in Assam. Laura, a medical doctor, had grown up in India. Arlene and she had corresponded as teenagers after Laura's parents, the Selanders, had spoken at Arlene's Harlan church, Bethel Baptist.

Ethel Hagstrom had also been raised in India by missionary parents. Ethel's brother Albert had kidnapped Arlene's fancy years before. She also knew several other mission members in Assam either from Harlan or St. Paul.

The following year, Arlene continued learning Assamese and served in the dispensary. "I was left alone a great deal during my second year and was extremely lonely." Work paid off. She passed her Second-Year Assamese Exam.

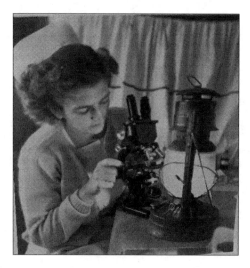

Nurse Arlene Jensen studying microscope slide by lantern-light in Assam.
(Family photo)

Christmas Eve Day of 1951, Arlene and several others met Betty Person at the Gauhati airport. "I had prayed that the Lord would send the nurse of his choosing to work with us," she recorded. God chose Betty, whom Arlene had taught at Mounds!

At the Christian Hospital in Gauhati, Arlene enrolled in a midwifery course. "I have been in charge of the maternity ward during this time and the experience of supervising the student nurses and informal teaching has been excellent for our future work in Tezpur." She gleefully announced that she and the other students had passed the oral and written exams and were now "government registered midwives, licensed to practice."

The mission constructed a dispensary in Tezpur, which opened in November. Patients eagerly arrived for medical help. And Arlene delighted in the work camaraderie with Nurse Betty Person and Drs. Merchant and Edwards.

Thirty-five to forty-five patients came for help each day with "middle ear infections, amebiasis, tuberculosis, gastric ulcers, skin diseases, malaria, along with an occasional Erb's palsy or diabetes. These keep us busy every day in our outpatient dispensary," Arlene enumerated. "Every morning before seeing anyone, Dr. Merchant holds a short service of Bible reading and prayer with those who have come. Then, each of us is in charge of a service one morning a week for those who are waiting. In one way or another, the Word goes out to those who seek physical help."

Inquirers in Iowa asked Bessie Olsen what items were needed for the prospective hospital. Arlene happily listed a desk and file for the nurses' office, beds, bassinettes, cribs, stretchers, mattresses, and so on.

In June, another Indian graduate nurse, Topeswari Doimari, joined the team.

Somehow, Arlene mustered the energy to write her weekly letter to her mother:

> I'm almost too tired to think. What a day this has been! At 8 a.m., I preached at the jail. Paul usually does it; but there was no man, so I had to go. It was in Assamese. It was a queer feeling to go way inside, having doors all locked behind. There were nineteen there. Imagine—Christians in prison. Then at 6 p.m., at the English Bible Class, I had to speak again, besides driving in and picking up a load of people. So, I'm tired, but thank the Lord that all went well.

Betty Person and Arlene crafted a joint letter to supporters in December of 1952:

> Our new evangelist has just arrived. His name is Motilol Bosu-mathari. As we work busily giving hypos, dressing sores, or helping the doctor as he stitches up a wound, we hear Motilol's voice from the nearby waiting room, telling the people stories of Jesus, using large picture rolls and reading to them from the Word of God. When he finishes his message, he sits down on the bench with those who are interested and talks with them a long as he has opportunity.

At first, predominantly Hindu patients came to the clinic, but then Muslims from the villages about ten miles away began coming. They arrived in groups of four or more, with their women hidden carefully behind curtains in oxcarts. The dispensary continued to bustle. From November 1952 through 1953, they treated 3,750 new patients.

Meanwhile, construction on the hospital, the nursing students' hostel, and doctors' housing took shape slowly. Intense anticipation marked the beginning of 1954. They had several applicants for the nursing school.

Arlene's friend and boss, Dan Danielson, Foreign Secretary of the Mission, let her know that he was resigning due to health concerns. A Rev. John Wilcox would take his place.

Missionaries Wilbur and Pearl Sorley worked with the Miri people group. These needed medical treatment. Dr. Laura Edwards and Arlene agreed to make the trek to the Miri with the Sorleys. Arlene wrote her mother about her adventure into India's back-country:

> We were supposed to take a boat, which wasn't there. So, we crossed the river in another boat. (It had started to rain.) I had my cold yet—hoarse and a cough. Had to wade half of the river and walked about three miles through freshly cut jungle and mud. We were still two miles from the Miri village we were going to; so, we stayed there and camped in a schoolhouse—an airy one. Next day, started out again. Still raining; but by the time we got to the village, it had stopped. There, Wilbur had a service and preached, while Laura saw about forty patients and I gave out medicines.
>
> We started back 2:30 or 3:30, walked two miles, then got a boat the rest of the way down and across the big river. In the meantime, a small stream we had driven over had become a raging torrent. Fortunately, the Jeep was on the other side, but it was hard to stay on your feet walking across in the dark by then. The road was muddy from so much rain, but we got safely home by 9 p.m. and my cold was no worse.

Work on the hospital compound kept everyone hopping. Arlene made a trip to Shillong to get a permit from the Director of Consumer Goods. They needed 150 bags of cement to finish the ring well and nurses' home; he approved fifty. Then, she flew to Calcutta to expedite orders for a water pump, paint, an examining table, and chairs.

Student nurses began arriving on the first of April. The thirteenth—a day to remember:

> Sunday, we had a day of prayer and dedication for our new hospital. We had continuous prayer, people coming and going from 6 a.m. to 12 noon. Then, at 2:30, a dedication service. With Christians from town and representatives from North Lakhimpur, Darrang, and [other areas]. It was really a thrill! We showed them around, although many things are left to be painted and finished up. The water tank is getting put up and the electric wires are being strung.

After years of dreaming, hoping, planning, and frantic work, the hospital at Tezpur officially opened for business on June 18, 1954. Now, patients could receive more extensive care than the dispensary could provide. One doctor was appointed Chief Medical Officer. Arlene received the responsibilities Superintendent of the Baptist Christian Hospital and Director of the Nursing School. This involved hearing morning reports, teaching students, rounds with the doctor, planning diets, dealing with hospital correspondence, ordering supplies, working in the outpatient department, monitoring expenditures and fees, "or a hundred other things." She reveled in this expanded ministry. A decade or so later she wrote:

> This was one of the most thrilling years of my life. To help initiate a completely new compound and medical program with no one else's mistakes to inherit, to work with Dr. Laura Edwards and Dr. Joseph Schoonmaker and Miss Betty Person and later five Indian graduate nurses was a rare privilege. We couldn't have been a happier team and I had a deeply satisfying sense of being exactly where the Lord wanted me to be. Though we saw very few conversions, a great deal of witnessing was carried out in spite of our busy program and we attempted to inspire the students, both men and women, to be concerned for the patients' souls as well as bodies.

Baptist Christian Hospital, Tespur, Assam, India, with staff and student nurses. Arlene Jensen fourth from left, ca. 1955.
(Photo curtesy of Converge)

A second class of nursing students began their studies in October. Bosunti, an Indian graduate nurse, enlarged the team. Arlene's letter to Bessie gave a snapshot of Oct. 26:

> From 5 a.m. on, it was an extremely busy day. I started a new class for the new students. We had to dig out White Cross blankets for patients today and we have some very sick ones: a man with a

bleeding ulcer—vomiting blood, one with a ruptured appendix—peritonitis, one operation for removal of an eye gouged out by a cow a month ago, then a tiny baby who can't keep food down. So, with all the rest—fourteen or so—it really keeps the nurses busy. I finally got home at 6 p.m. to my birthday party.

Arlene had also trained Ruby Eliason at Mounds-Midway. Ruby arrived in Assam in late December. With Arlene's furlough approaching in late spring of 1955, she prepared Nurse Eliason to replace her.

January brought more cold weather. Arlene admitted, "To go into the operating room and take off two sweaters and scrub your hands and arms to the elbows for ten minutes in a cold, cement operating room with a cement floor is rather shivery!"

She made the mistake of telling her mother that she had seen a tiger as she and Ruby walked between villages. "This time of year, it's so dry and tigers are hungry and coming closer to houses. The villages are having a hard time. Tigers are getting many cows and pigs." Later, she tried to set Bessie's mind at rest. "We all really had a laugh at your worrying about the tigers. I didn't mean to worry you. Actually, we aren't in much more danger of being attacked than you are. I've been dying to see one ever since coming here and even though it was small, it was real."

All rejoiced in April at receiving certification for eighteen months from the Nursing School Association for their new school.

The time for Arlene's furlough drew near. "Wow! Do I dislike farewells! It's going to be hard for me to leave here. I can hardly stand to think of it and yet am so anxious to get home, too." She exalts, "Praise the Lord, I got my 'No Objection to Return,' so now an all set with the Police for leaving. Yesterday, the Tezpur church farewelled me. I got a lovely Assamese costume."

On May 5, she recorded, "Monday, everyone practically went to the airport—from the gardeners to the nurses and missionaries—42 in all!"

Her trek homeward took her by Addis Ababa to visit friends in Ethiopia who had formerly worked in Assam, then to Denmark. There she tried to connect with some of her father's and stepfather's families.

She finally arrived in Denver, Colorado, in June, in time for a Board of Foreign Missions program that included furloughed missionaries. Her good friends the Danielsons and Merchants were present. The newly appointed Foreign Missions Secretary, John Wilcox, brought a message of inspiration.

While Arlene was thrilled to reach home and loved ones, India still called to her.

CHAPTER 18

The Hashemite Kingdom and the Heavenly Kingdom

1951

M ERREL met royalty on his first visit to Jordan when he had accompanied the pregnant Bahraini widow there. "I remember how thrilled I was when Dr. McLean took me to the palace in Amman and introduced me to King Abdullah, who was so very friendly and helpful."

But nine days before the Callaways took flight for Jordan, "at the door of the mosque in Jerusalem, the King was assassinated for being too moderate toward Israel," Merrel said.

Sometime after the Callaways arrived in Ajloun in August 1951, Merrel said, "I was again taken to the palace and introduced to Abdullah's son, the new King [Talal]; but he soon went tragically out of his mind. As for Abdullah's grandson, Hussein, who witnessed his grandfather's assassination," Merrel quipped later, "I moved . . . hoping to ensure him a long and healthy life and reign!"

Those comments aside, Merrel explained, "Ajloun is a village located about two- or three-hours' drive from Amman. Since I will be the only missionary evangelist in town, I will have charge of the hospital services, be pastor, and try eventually to organize believers into a church, as well as oversee the operation of a small school."

Merrel Callaway and Dr. Charles McLean in Ajloun, Jordan, with twelfth century Ajloun Castle in distance, ca. 1951.
(Photo courtesy of the International Mission Board, SBC)

The Southern Baptist Foreign Mission Board had built a small house and clinic about forty miles from Ajloun for the McLeans and a nurse. McLean returned it to the Foreign Mission Board on his retirement. Later, Finlay Graham studied Arabic in that house.

Another mission also faced financial woes after World War II. Impressed with the medical work in Ajloun, they invited the Southern Baptist Convention to take over their Gaza hospital.

The Callaways moved into a two-story house shaded by an olive tree. The twelfth-century Muslim Ajloun Castle brooded over the town on a hilltop. Construction workers erected buildings across the compound, with hammers constantly ringing out their rhythmical beat. A tiny bakery produced the round flatbread by slamming it against heated walls. Camel caravans plodded leisurely through the town. Chickens squabbled around their coop and the Callaway youngsters played with the winsome goat kids. The three daughters enjoyed reconnecting with Vangy, their Palestinian *aiyah*, (nursemaid), now training as a nurse.

Susan Callaway plays with kid; Joy, Sharon, and Jordanian lady join the fun, ca. 1951.
(Family photo)

Merrel ministered as hospital chaplain and spiritual mentor to local Christians and expatriates. Fellowship with their good friends Lorne and Gin Brown and their girls, Dr. August Lovegren and wife, Alta Lee, the nursing and hospital support staff, and local friends blessed their lives.

Beth became pregnant with their fourth child.

Shortly before her delivery date, Merrel spoke Easter Sunday morning at Gordon's Tomb (or the Garden Tomb, as it was also called) in Jerusalem. Some Christians consider this tomb outside the old city walls the possible place of Jesus' burial. In Merrel's sunrise service message, he identified himself with Barabbas. The Jewish mob had screamed at Pilate to set free this prisoner instead of Jesus during Passover week. The Messiah sacrificed his life on Calvary for Merrel and for "whosoever"; hence his sermon title, "I Am Barabbas."

Baby Star or *Nijma*, a common Jordanian name for girls, arrived safely. The post-delivery went poorly. Drs. Lorne Brown and Gus Lovegren struggled to control Beth's bleeding. The new father recalls Lorne's visit the next morning. "He came over to my house saying that he had spent the night searching his medical books, because he had been unable to stop the mother's bleeding." Star holds the honor as the first missionary child of the Baptist Mission to be born at the Ajloun Baptist Hospital, as they renamed it.

When the Callaways had first arrived in Palestine in 1945, they met Mona and Raymond Joyce, missionaries to China. Due to the political situation in China, the Joyces had been forced to leave. On their way back to their native Canada, they stopped in Jerusalem. Raymond secured a job post there in the Bishop's (Church of England's) school for young men. The Anglican Cathedral was near the Callaways' hostel. "Being kindred spirits," Merrel said, "Joyce invited me to speak at chapel one day. As we talked, he said, 'We're going back to Canada to try to start a chapter of the Fellowship of Faith for Muslims.'"

Merrel summarized what he had learned about how Fellowship of Faith for Muslims had begun years before:

> During the Keswick Annual Conference in the Lake District of England, under giant tents, Samuel Zwemer talked up the need in neglected Arabia from Muscat to Kuwait. He spoke on the text, "Master, we have toiled all the night and taken nothing: nevertheless, at thy word, I will let down the net" [Luke 5:8]. People were so moved that at least 500 remained in their seats after the service. The sermon inspired them to form the Fellowship of Faith for Muslims, an organization of those who believed that Muslims could be saved. On the spot, they elected Zwemer as honorary president.
>
> The Canadian told me the FFM even had a library for missionaries to borrow books for their work and send out prayer letters. He gave me some literature and I attended their annual meeting in London. I felt that it should not be bottled up in Canada, but should be in [the United States], too, where it would have a lot more chance of getting people praying.

But now Beth and Merrel served in Jordan. They remembered the mighty way God had moved in their Jerusalem days, when Christians there had all joined in prevailing prayer. Revival had come to hearts. They wondered if this could not happen among the myriads of searching Muslims, if only American Christians would storm heaven with their pleas.

The two seriously searched for God's leading. Should they stay and continue the work they had begun in Ajloun? Or would they be more effective securing American prayer partners for the salvation of hurting hearts? They also had to consider that Beth still had not regained her health since giving birth.

They talked with the Middle East Secretary of the Foreign Mission Board. "Dr. Sadler said that if I was sure this was the Lord's will, he was all for it; but I'd have to separate from the Board. I knew that to bring FFM to the States, I'd have to get on the ball and start doing it and resign. So, we did."

Their time in Ajloun did have eternal effect. Many moons later Merrel told, "I met an Arab speaker at a 'World Missions Conference.' He publicly mentioned a time in Jordan when Lorne Brown and I visited in his home and he accepted Christ as his Savior. Yes, this man from our medical base in Jordan is now reaching Arabic-speaking Muslims in the USA." Merrel added, "I believe I got the Lord's will in leaving the Southern Baptists. They profited from the prayer angle of this thing."

Saying goodbye to friends old and new is seldom easy. "In a taxi to the airport and America," Merrel remembers, "we were singing, 'Trav'ling home, trav'ling home, led by Jesus we are trav'ling home.'"[1]

When the SS *Independence* docked in the US harbor, her parents carried Star off the ship in a wicker laundry basket. The family settled again in Bloomfield. No longer with the Foreign Mission Board, they trusted God to meet their monetary needs. After a time, Merrel wrote his family on James Island:

> For the past five months, Beth and I have been trying to stir up interest in a missionary union and information service for the Muslim world, called the Fellowship of Faith for Muslims. The Lord is blessing and our headquarters indicates more interest in the Muslim World than ever before. As you know, the FFM is not a money-raising organization in the sense that it pays salaries, etc. It is a labor of love by different missionaries who are connected with other organizations.
>
> Beth and I believe that God is now enlarging our opportunity in the spheres of evangelism, Bible teaching, and foreign missions. We have been called to lead the work of the Evangelistic Committee of Newark and Vicinity. This powerful evangelistic and missionary agency has been a mighty force for good in the New York–New Jersey metropolitan area and to the ends of the earth.

As Director of the Newark Evangelistic Committee, Merrel recalls:

> I saw that as an opportunity to bring Raymond Joyce down from Canada and show his stereoptical slides of his work in the Muslim part of Inner Mongolia. Raymond was to speak at the big TNT Rally [for young people]; but I got Bill Miller, who was the best evangelist among Muslims in Iran, to talk to the ladies about

1. Harkness, "Traveling Home." In the public domain.

missions to Muslims. I got Christie Wilson Sr. to come from Princeton. He'd been a missionary to Muslims, also in Iran. Getting these men together is what brought the FFM to the US. Now, Doris and Bob Schneider [former missionaries to the Arab/Berber world] run one of the most active FFM chapters near Chicago.

In another letter, Merrel asked his family to pray "for Beth's physical well-being. It looks as though she must undergo an operation. It is good that the Lord has arranged it so that she can be near a very fine New York specialist at this time."

Osteomyelitis reoccurred in nine-year-old Sharon's tibia. She spent her summer in and out of Doctors Hospital for treatment. Beth also stayed there off and on for medical help.

The doctors finally diagnosed Beth with aleukemic leukemia. Blood tests had failed to reveal increased white blood cells. Labor Day week, staff admitted her again to the hospital where her father worked as Director of Operations. There she received treatment from the best specialists available. About thirteen individuals donated blood for her. The Fountains invited the Callaways to stay at their home during their daughter Elizabeth's hospitalization.

Sharon, too, underwent another bone operation and they again encased her lower leg in a cast.

Home on furlough, the Lorne Browns came by Beth's hospital room while her children were there. The Brown daughters and Beth's girls chattered away with each other in Arabic. Time had not dimmed their friendship.

The doctor told Merrel that Beth could not possibly return to the mission field in the next year or so, if ever. With this information, Merrel accepted a call as pastor to Calvary Baptist Church in Macon, Georgia, effective the beginning of December. Merrel went on ahead to Macon, intending to bring his wife down there after Christmas.

Despite the top medical help America could offer, Beth's body succumbed to the leukemia. With her last words, she prayed for her sister Joyce's salvation. Early on the morning of Wednesday, December 23, 1953, Elizabeth Fountain Callaway's dear Savior welcomed her home to his heavenly kingdom.

Elizabeth Fountain Callaway
(Photo courtesy of the International Mission Board, SBC)

"The young doctor told me she had died," Merrel later said, "and motioned for me to follow him out into the hall, at the end of which he sat in front of a tremendous window on the hospital's fourteenth floor. He pointed to the County Hospital a block or so away and began shouting, 'You see those guys? You can't kill them! They're a bunch of drunks and dope fiends and you can't kill them!'"

In his own grief, did Merrel question or blame God for taking his beloved wife from him? Did he wonder down the years why the mother of his children had been stripped from their family? Family and friends did hear him often voice this thought: "I just hope that that doctor didn't get so mad at God that I don't see him in heaven someday. If I do, I'll tell him, 'If God does something you don't understand, don't ask, "Why?" Ask, "What—what are you doing, Lord?"'"

As Merrel made his way back to New Jersey, did he register the ringing of collection bells or the Yuletide carols booming across the airwaves? Did he even notice the intricate department store displays or take in the holiday decorations festooning the city?

He reached the Fountains' home on Long Hill and settled his girls on the rose-pink Duncan-Phyfe loveseat in the parlor. First, he asked them to be very brave. Then he shared that their mother had died and was even now in heaven with Jesus.

Both Merrel's father and sister Gyp boarded trains for New Jersey the next morning. Pastor Weber, assisted by T.W. Callaway and two of Guion's minister brothers, led the service at Long Hill Chapel. T.W. wrote the CCC, "While there was sadness, yet there was 'the peace of God that passeth understanding' [Philippians 4:7] in every heart. The funeral Saturday afternoon was simple and very impressive." Beth's earthly tent was interred in the Fountain family section of Hillside Cemetery in Plainfield, covered by a simple plaque.

Telegrams, cards, and letters of shock, condolence, and comfort flowed to Merrel and into the Fountain home. Tributes and memories about Beth included, "a person of delicate beauty and charm"; "such a vivacious and radiant girl"; "All came to love Beth. Her deep spiritual life with its radiant spirit made an everlasting impression on everyone"; "Hers was a great faith, lighting the path and pointing the way for many who shall have the Abundant Life because she lived." At least fifteen Christian women's and youth groups in nine different states renamed their organizations in her memory, not to mention the Beth Callaway Young Women's Auxiliaries in Georgia and Virginia.

In lieu of flowers, Merrel requested donations to a Beth Callaway Memorial Schools Fund. Trustees earmarked the fund for three possible ministries in the Arab world: a school for children of missionaries, a New East Bible College, and a Bible Conference Center. Since Merrel had four children and Virginia and Lorne Brown now had three, they agreed that the school for missionaries' children must come first.

But what to do now about Merrel's own children? How could he minister at his pastorate in Macon and still adequately care for his four youngsters? Sharon was almost ten, with yet another leg surgery looming; Star, a little over a year-and-a-half old; and Susan and Joy sandwiched between them. Relatives suggested splitting the sisters up, taking one to each of their houses. Merrel told of an offer from one of Beth's cousins:

> Out in California, she wrote to Gramma Fountain and said, "Look, we couldn't take all four girls; but the oldest, Sharon, we could cope with somebody that old. So, would you ask Merrel about that possibility?"
>
> Thank goodness, the Lord gave me the right answer right off and for the right reason. I said, "Well, Gramma, there'll come a day when those girls will need each other much more than they'll need me or somebody else, when they'll mean more to one another;

'cause you and I, Gramma, won't be around forever, so I want them to stick together."

Callaway daughters
from left, back **Sharon, Susan**
from left, front **Joy, Star**
(Family photo)

Merrel stayed in Jersey for two or three weeks after the funeral, then moved his family down to Macon. His mother's sister, Aunt Arnee Lebby, came from James Island and looked after the children for at least a month. Gyp drove down from Knoxville to help out for a time, as did the Fountains. At bedtime, the girls ended their prayers, " . . . and bless Mummy up in heaven."

Merrel's oldest sister, Mirvin, and her husband Jack Jackson and teenage son Jackie then moved to Macon. Regarding Jack Sr. Merrel said:

> He became my assistant pastor. And he took over the business side of the Beth Callaway Memorial Schools Fund—all the correspondence, all the thanking people for gifts, making sure the finances could be represented to the fund's trustees. [These] were Grampa Fountain and Dr. Wingblade of Trinity Baptist Church, where I went to church in New York City when Beth was sick. Dr. Wingblade had been President of Bethel Baptist College and Seminary in St. Paul. I had to answer to them. And me, we were the three trustees. I didn't have to worry about the money that

came in. Jack Jackson kept all that straight. He liberated me for my speaking engagements.

Calvary Baptist Church welcomed the Callaways. A paragraph under a picture of Beth in a springtime Sunday bulletin read, "Beth's serious illness prevented her coming to Calvary with Merrel when he became our pastor. Although she never came to Calvary, her membership was placed with us along with Merrel's and she lives in our midst at all times."

Life in Georgia was pleasant, especially when the sweet scent of invasive honeysuckle vines filled the air. But finding someone to look after the girls on an ongoing basis proved difficult. In September, Gram Fountain registered the three older daughters in Macon public schools.

Then, Guion and Florence approached Merrel with a sacrificial offer. By now in their sixties, they suggested that all four children live with them in New Jersey for an indefinite time. This meant lonelier times for Merrel, but he saw this as the most workable solution for the present. After one week of Georgia schools, the three enrolled in the Chatham Township schools. They had lived with Gram and Gramp the previous fall, so the change was not dramatic. Merrel continued shepherding his church in Macon.

"But then," he explained, "I received a letter from the Dahran Protestant Fellowship in Saudi Arabia, looking to ask me to come as their pastor. I wrote them, 'Sorry, but the Lord's will, these four little girls . . .' I just didn't feel it was the Lord's will. But it did start me thinking, 'Maybe there's some way I can get back into foreign missions.'"

Merrel informed his church that he was resigning his pastorate effective November 1, 1954. A news clipping stated, "A motion requesting him to reconsider his resignation was unanimously passed by the church."

Nevertheless, he and the Jackson family settled in Jersey. Merrel stayed with his girls on Long Hill, the Jacksons in nearby Madison. From there Merrel promoted the Beth Callaway Memorial Schools Fund and the need for Muslims to hear of God's love for them. He spoke in churches and venues across the country. He gave Arabic lessons to prospective missionaries. His brother-in-law Jack continued to deal with the business side of the fund. Mirvin gave nieces Sharon and Susan piano lessons and sometimes looked after Star.

Merrel found the perfect opportunity for promoting missions and awareness of the Beth Callaway Memorial Schools Fund. He hoped to set up a booth at the Urbana Student Missions Conference scheduled for five days in December in Champaign-Urbana, Illinois. InterVarsity Christian

Fellowship sponsored this massive student gathering every few years to inform college students of mission opportunities, issues, and needs. Merrel wanted Guion, as a fund trustee, to allow him to borrow money from it to pay for his trip. Merrel described what ensued:

> Guion's too good a businessman to go for that. He said, "No, but I'll lend you the money for such a trip, but you can't touch the fund." I knew he was right and I just forgot about Urbana.
>
> But then, waiting on the Lord instead of getting mad at Grampa, what should come but a letter from a Jewish girl, whom Beth and I had known at Harvard! We were in InterVarsity there together. When she became a Christian, her psychiatric father (I think both her mother and her father were psychiatrists) —Jewish—I think they practically disowned her.
>
> When we lived in Ajloun, I made a trip to Beirut. She was living with some lady British missionaries. It was all women-folk. I did go by and ask if she was there. They said, "No, she's not here," so I didn't get to see her.
>
> She had gotten on the BCMSF mailing list somehow. She asked if I would come and speak at this big prayer meeting at Moody Bible Institute just before classes begin in a big lecture room.
>
> That night at supper, she asked, "Did you ever stop by that mission in Beirut and ask if I was there?"
>
> I said, "Yes, and they said you weren't there at that time."
>
> "I was there and they didn't let me know, because you were a man, an American man."
>
> They didn't know her loyalty to Beth and to us. That triggered her leaving and she came on the staff at Moody.
>
> After I spoke there at the prayer meeting, someone showed me the 102 building where my daddy had roomed in 1901, two doors down from Dwight L. Moody's office. I was free about ten o'clock. Then, I got to thinking, "Now, who do I know in Chicago besides this girl who had invited me? Well, I know one person— John Wilcox."
>
> At the time Sharon was born, I was pastor at Alexander Park, VA, and John Wilcox was over in Norfolk at a new church that was growing like wildfire. He was a member of the Baptist Ministers' Conference, Norfolk and Portsmouth being together. He had a real passion for foreign missions. We were just kindred spirits from the word go.
>
> Consequently, I went on to the mission field. He had a deacon in that church, who was from Chicago, who had been a member

of Addison Street Baptist Church, between a big Swedish community and Cubs Stadium. When his deacon went back to Addison, his home church, they needed a pastor. He said, "I know just the man!" They called Wilcox.

So, I thought of John Wilcox. We'd been great friends, but hadn't seen one another in over five years. John answered, "Ruby says to come out for lunch." They asked me about my situation. I told them about my four little girls living with their grandparents. By the end of the meal, he said, "Let me make you an offer."

CHAPTER 19

"Whither Thou Goest"

1955

LUNCH over, John Wilcox confided to Merrel, "You know, I guess I was too missionary-minded, because when the Secretary for the Foreign Mission Board of the Swedish Baptists, now the Baptist General Conference, retired, they chose me to succeed him. But I've never been a foreign missionary. But you have, so I want you to be my Administrative Assistant.

"John knew I could compose a letter and take it into his office to sign without his having to change a thing," Merrel clarified, "because we saw eye to eye on missions."

"I promise you," Wilcox bargained, "that every third week, I'll give you a long weekend in New Jersey with your children and their grandparents. Furthermore, I'll give you a full two-week holiday to take those children down to James Island and Fernandina Beach."

Merrel agreed. He settled into work in Chicago at Baptist General Conference Mission Headquarters. "One of my jobs was to send a letter from the Board to these missionaries arriving home to the States, a pass so they could ride free (like an ordained minister) on the railroads, and a check to cover expenses [to their destination]. If they came through Chicago when John wasn't available, it was my job to introduce them to people in the head office."

The following summer, Merrel griped:

> We arrived on James Island and were just enjoying things fine, planning sometime the second week to take [the girls] down to Fernandina Beach. I was very angry when I received this letter

saying, "Look, we're having an outgoing and furloughing missions conference at Woodlake, Wisconsin. You've *got* to come speak at it during that week."

I was so mad! Wilcox broke his promise! And I was frustrated, looking forward to Fernandina with my kids. Instead, I had to drop them at Long Hill, Chatham, NJ, and go on to Woodlake.

One of the furloughing missionaries there was Arlene Jensen, who had just finished her five-and-a-half years in Assam, India. (I hadn't seen her [in Chicago], but had sent her the [welcoming] letter and all that and had signed my name. I got something in my eye, maybe sand from the lake. Knowing she was a nurse, I walked up to her. "Look, there's something wrong with my eye."

She said, "Oh, it's just some dust," and brushed it off as though it was nothing.

People were asking about this new speaker, Merrel Callaway. The name "Callaway" sounded odd, definitely not Scandinavian. Word went out that he was a returned widowed missionary with four young daughters. Arlene tried to stay clear of him! She wanted to resume her medical work at the new hospital in Tezpur.

At the close of the conference, the conferees loaded into cars over the weekend to attend a foreign missions rally at a church in Minneapolis. Many of them would speak at the service. They spruced up in the rooms behind the platform. Merrel caught sight of Arlene looking so attractive in her Indian sari and Arlene thought she noticed a glint of interest in his eyes. When she came out on stage, she scanned the audience for a glimpse of him, but somehow missed him sitting on the second row.

That night, John and Merrel rode back on the train together to Chicago. Their conversation drifted to women, Merrel recalls:

I said, "What do you think of Arlene Jensen?"

He said, "Oh, she's precious; she's precious!" So that didn't discourage me.

Arlene traveled from state to state and city to city, telling congregations about the mission work being done in Assam. She described the new hospital and the nursing school for Indian nationals.

On October 4, she received a telegram from Ruby Eliason and Betty Person regarding the state exam her first class of nursing students had just taken: "=all passed praise the lord=ruby betty=."

A poignantly positive letter from an Assamese friend arrived for her that fall:

Arlene, I missed you so much, especially your frank, open spiritual drive. Others [in Tezpur] had to curb their expressions of "When Arlene was here"; "If only Arlene were here." One time, in a matter of letting nurses wander over the bazaar, [someone] asked, "Would Miss Jensen have allowed this?" [The respondent] shook his head, smiling knowingly, 'Never"; then he paused and added the biggest compliment a Superintendent of Nurses could ever have: "Miss Jensen was firm, but she was also very kind."

Besides doing deputation work, Arlene took Nursing Administration at the University of Minnesota one quarter. She enrolled in two courses at Bethel Bible College and Seminary on Church History and on New Testament Theology. Her thesis in Church History focused on the persecution in Lutheran Denmark that her Baptist grandparents had suffered. At that time, her grandmother had had to sneak out of her house prior to dawn and break the ice to be baptized.

Other furloughed missionary women also enrolled at Bethel. Merrel routinely wrote to them regarding mission business. Arlene finally asked one of her friends, "Does Mr. Callaway sign your letters this way: 'With all very, very best wishes'?"

"No, he doesn't," came the quick reply.

Writing her life history for a job application a decade later, Arlene confessed:

> I was not interested in any man with four daughters. I had given my life for the Tezpur Hospital and Nursing School, so I avoided him carefully. I had been made aware of the problem of finishing one career prematurely by stories of a missionary nurse who married and spent a frustrated life hoping to return and never able to do so.
>
> However, over the next few months, through many detailed evidences of the Lord's leading, Merrel first, and I later, came to the conclusion that my calling was to be changed to that of his wife and the mother of his children. Even up until this time, there was nothing I wanted less than to be a stepmother. The end of January, I told my Board Secretary that I was willing to return anytime without finishing my furlough.

Somehow, Mr. and Mrs. Wilcox and Merrel and Arlene ended up dining at a restaurant together. Deftly, Ruby and John managed to give the other two time to chat together privately for a while.

The gossip mill churned. Betty Person, home on medical leave, nosed around. Her December 11, 1955, letter queried, "Say, what are you holding out on us? Merchants say you have some pretty nice friends. What's the deal? You know they're all waiting for you back in Tezpur and needing your help."

Ruby Eliason on the same date bluntly wrote, "How's your love life? We are dying to know! Just a scant word here and there has made us curious."

When Arlene came to Mission Headquarters, Merrel met her train. As usual, he led her on a tour of the headquarters and introduced her to new staff. In his own office, she noticed the picture of his four daughters. Later, she admitted, "It was love at first sight."

Cupid got cracking in February. Merrel recounts:

> Arlene had left her lap typewriter at Headquarters for someone to fix. Wilcox got me a speaking engagement around St. Paul, where she was going to Bethel Seminary. Since I was going, I was asked to take the typewriter. Early that Sunday afternoon, I gave her the typewriter. She invited me to go with her to a little church on the edge of St. Paul, where she had to speak at 5:30. I heard her speak and was impressed.
>
> By the time we got back into town from church, I stopped by the Hamline Hotel on N. Snelling Avenue and said, "Why don't we go see what the lobby is like?" In the lobby, I pulled the ring out of my pocket and she accepted it.

In true Merrel style, he later wisecracked, "I slipped the disc onto her digit."

T.W. Callaway's birthday arrived for the eighty-second time. Merrel wrote his father:

> Here is your "Happy Birthday" present—another lovely daughter-in-law-to-be. Yes, I am engaged to be married. This proves that your baby boy loves you most, because he's giving you twice as many daughters as the other Callaway kids.
>
> Her name is Arlene Jensen. Served one term in Tezpur, As-sam, India, as a missionary nurse and teacher of Indian nurses in training at the hospital and nurses's school of the Baptist General Conference of America. She loves Jesus, just like Beth did. We are separated for the month of March, while Arlene does deputation work for the Foreign Mission Board out in California. However, I will see her at Easter.

A month later, Merrel let his father know that they would be married at Bethel Baptist Church in Harlan, Iowa, the evening of May 25:

> This week, Arlene is in Alaska. Am enclosing a small photo of Arlene. (She is sho' pretty, Pop!) Last week, the children had their spring vacation from school. So, Arlene went to Chatham, NJ, and had a nice visit with the Fountains and the children one night. Then Mr. Fountain took her and Sharon and Susan to the airport in New York, so that the three could fly to Chicago. Sharon and Susan had a nice week visiting the two daughters of Rev. and Mrs. John Wilcox here; then I took them back to Chatham on the train last night.

Earlier, Merrel had told Florence and Guion about his engagement. He was nervous about their reaction to the news. "When I wrote the Fountains about Arlene," he later said, "Gram sent me a lovely letter, saying that, of course, having lost her daughter, nobody could replace Beth in her heart; but I was afraid that when Arlene descended upon New Jersey, how could they not resent her?"

Actually, the Fountains' main concern was that he might marry a light-headed flibbertigibbet who would not properly care for their granddaughters. When they did meet Arlene, they were relieved at how "settled" she was. As she rolled into their driveway, she spied Star dancing around on the big front porch. "There's my little darling!" she exclaimed with delight.

T.W., along with each of his children, penned a welcoming letter to Arlene May 30:

> As head of the "Callaway Clan," we gladly welcome you as the latest member of the CCC. We are honored with your membership. You will find them a jolly and loving lot, serving the Lord.
>
> We already love you for taking pity upon that lonely Merrel. With all his faults, we love him still; but we feel certain you will learn to overlook them. Our hearts and homes are yours and bushels of love for the newly initiated member of the Clan.

On May 10 Aunt Arnee sent heartfelt greetings also:

> When I left Meck's home in Macon two years ago this month, my constant prayer has been that God would provide a "helpmate" for him and a truly Christian mother for his children. When Bro. Callaway read to me Meck's first letter, telling about Arlene, I gave a shout of joy and thanksgiving!

> Now, I want to welcome Arlene into the Royall-Lebby side
> of the Callaway Clan. Since I am the oldest in this branch of the
> family, I claim a kind of matriarchal privilege to speak for all the
> others.

The couple planned to marry "on a shoestring" due to almost non-existent finances. But loved ones produced a stunning wedding gown for Arlene, flowers for the church, and a three-tiered cake for the reception in the church fellowship hall. Arlene's sisters Margaret and Hulda served as her matron of honor and bridesmaid. The newlyweds spent one brief night in Omaha, Nebraska, before attempting to finish their honeymoon in Chicago.

Merrel described the change in plans. "I had wondered about the complete acceptance by Grandma and I didn't know Aunt Joy's position; 'cause, after all, she was Beth's sister. But on our honeymoon, we received a letter from Joy Fountain, saying that Grampa had had a heart attack and had to go into the hospital. Gram had also to go in. Could Arlene come out immediately? We put her on a plane and she was there the next day. So Arlene went back, not as an intruder, but as a female equivalent to a knight in shining armor, saving the day.

Before their wedding, Merrel had applied to the Baptist General Conference Foreign Mission Board as a prospective missionary. Perhaps he and Arlene could continue her work in Tezpur or maybe they could join the new medical outreach among the Danakil in Eritrea, Africa. The Board's decision shocked and devastated Arlene:

> At the annual meeting in June, we were told that he would not be
> appointed, because the "issue was too confused." This was a great
> disappointment to me at the time; in fact, it rocked my world! But
> I knew that, as a small denomination with a new foreign mission
> program, the main problems had been with missionaries coming
> to them from other Boards. As time went on, I came to realize the
> wisdom of this decision in our own lives.
>
> In July, the children came to live with us—Sharon 12, Susan
> 10, Joy almost 8, and Star 4. We traveled most of the summer, set-
> tling down in the fall in Andover Lake, Connecticut, while Merrel
> attended the Kennedy School of Missions in Hartford.

Due to donations from a Kennedy, the Hartford Seminary Foundation had established the Kennedy School of Missions. The funds provided a much-needed scholarship for Merrel.

Merrel's father had deeded him a waterfront piece of land with a small cottage on Clark Sound, South Carolina. Merrel sold the empty west half of the lot to his sister Kate and her husband, Luther Osment. The $200 a month from that sale paid the Callaways' rent on the red two-bedroom bungalow across the road from the lake. Merrel's speaking engagements brought in some cash.

Ups and downs accompanied the next nine months of adjustment to a new family situation. One day, Star asked her father about a "wicked step-mother." He banned the book *Cinderella* from the house.

As a former Director of Nursing and Hospital Supervisor with her own Indian cook, Arlene's life changed dramatically. Now she cooked and supervised four young girls, while her husband immersed himself in Islamic a.id Arabic studies an hour away.

When a neighbor learned of Arlene's pregnancy, she knitted a sweater for the little one.

Arlene confided later, "We wanted to return to the mission field, but how to find the Lord's will? I asked the Lord to help me win at least one soul, as a sign that he could use me and us on the mission field. I had the joy of seeing three decisions that winter in a children's Bible Club I had, assisted by my daughters."

While at the Kennedy School of Missions, Merrel renewed his acquaintance with a brilliant student, R. Marston Speight, whom he had briefly encountered at Columbia Bible College years before. Marston, his wife, Elizabeth, and their son, Jonathan, planned to return as missionaries to Morocco, North Africa.

Arlene described what happened next. "One day while walking across the campus, Marston told Merrel that his Mission, the Gospel Missionary Union, had a Conference Center in Morocco, a Bible School—temporarily closed, and was very much in need of personnel and funds for a school for missionaries' children. This impressed Merrel very much, because a memorial fund for his first wife had been started for one of these projects. And he was expected to be part of the project."

After much prayer, investigation, and deliberation, Arlene and Merrel applied to go to Morocco under the Gospel Missionary Union with the intention of starting a school for missionaries' children. They knew of no such school in the Middle East or North Africa. Parents in those regions would have to send their children much farther for their education, spend the massive time homeschooling, or retire from the field.

The Callaways planned to travel to the Mission Headquarters in down-town Kansas City, Missouri, that summer. They would be evaluated by the Board and get to know the staff and their expectations. As a faith mission, employees were required to raise their own support. Missionaries could not leave for the field until they had been assured five years of financial support.

The Fountains were concerned and wrote Merrel ("not as a son-in-law, but as a son") a frank but kind and honest letter on May 19, 1957:

> We had hoped (as we think your father did, too) that you would now settle down to a church in this country or teach—because of the uncertainty on the mission field and for the sake of the children, who have been unsettled now for some time. This is a tremendous step you are contemplating, involving a great deal of effort and money and affecting the future welfare of the children.
>
> Do you feel confident at your age that you can learn Arabic now, which will be a new Arabic in Morocco? If you add learning French to that, it would be much more of a burden . . . .
>
> We certainly do not want to appear to be standing in the way of the Lord's work in any way, but we do like to give you our thoughts.

Merrel appreciated their frankness. But Merrel and Arlene felt that God had clearly opened a door in an amazing way to fulfill the ministry needs specified in the Beth Callaway Memorial Schools Fund. That summer, the two adults and Star settled into the front seat of their gray Dodge. The three older girls sat atop suitcases in the back seat, while their pink chenille bedspreads blocked the window sun. They whiled away the many hours braiding bedspread fringes, singing choruses, hymns, and silly songs, and playing license plate games. Merrel drove.

A month in Chicago, a visit to Gramma Olsen in Harlan, and a six-week stint at the Gospel Missionary Union Headquarters in boiling-hot Kansas City kept them busy. The Mission Board accepted Arlene and Merrel as their missionaries. The two would now need to raise their financial support. They made plans to sail for Morocco early in 1958.

The six then headed for South Carolina in late July. They had logged about four thousand travel miles that summer.

Arlene said, "I had a miscarriage at the end of our long trip; which was a disappointment to me, because I wanted just one baby of my own."

T.W. communicated, "Dear CCC, Merrel and family are with me. We have all fallen desperately in love with Arlene. She is a dear, sweet Christian girl and proves an excellent mother to Meck's four girls." He mentioned that most of the Clan were there off and on, with twenty or more sitting down together for meals three times a day. Grits figured prominently for breakfast. A platoon of Army cots squatted side by side with military precision on the cottage's concrete basement floor.

The six spent that fall on James Island. T.W. and Merrel shared tender times together, often relaxing on the green porch swing. Age and blood pressure were taking its toll on the older man. Time, though, never dimmed his indomitable spirit. He called his daily medicine dose "The Old Dead Mule."

The children sent letters to their Jersey grandparents. Susan especially thanked them for her increased allowance. Joy wrote, "When Susan found out she was going to get a dollar for her allowance, she yelled. I thought she would lose her voice, she yelled so loud." Star loved learning at a Baptist church kindergarten. And Sharon's school crowned her "Snow Princess." Merrel charged her Uncle Luther with bringing her home right after the awards ceremony and definitely before the dancing started. He fudged a little.

Merrel and Arlene audited a French class at the College of Charleston to prepare for life in Morocco. While this North African country had won its independence from France the year before, French remained the language of business and commerce.

Mirvin and Jack Jackson and Roy and Ruby Callaway had recently built one-story homes on Cherry Lane, one and two houses down from the cottage. (Brother Royall remains famous in the family for having baptized young Jimmy Carter in his church at Plains, Georgia.) Mirvin resumed piano lessons with Susan and Sharon and started Joy on the musical path.

Late in December, T.W. and Merrel said their farewells. They would not see each other again this side of glory. T.W. often spouted, "I'm not looking for the undertaker; I'm looking for the Upper-Taker."

The family headed for Chatham and lived with the Fountains until their ship sailed. Florence and Guion called Arlene their daughter-in-law, which made her feel a real part of their family. Merrel often called her "Arlin' Darlin'" or "*Mein Chotsey.*"

The Callaways booked passage on the *Tekla Torm*, a Danish freighter.[1] Gramp rented a Cadillac limousine to drive them all to the ship docked at

---

1. This author recounts her memories of the family's ship adventure. Some of this information was also published in an article: Joy Callaway Godbold, "One Dark Night," in *The Commission*, 51.

Hoboken on January 28, 1958. Hugs and kisses over, the four granddaughters and their parents boarded the ship. They waved goodbye to the beloved pair standing alone on the dock.

Sharon shortly afterward penned them a postcard. "Dear All, We are now on the boat waiting to sail. The ship is supposed to leave at about 6:00 p.m. We have two cabins, three persons in each. There is a small lounge and a small dining room. Most of the cargo, by the looks of loading, is oil and tractors. Susan, Joy, and Star have made friends with the captain and are exploring the whole ship. (Sailing time has changed to 9 p.m.)"

The sailing delay may have been caused by the giant wave that careened over the side of *Tekla Torm* before she even passed the Stature of Liberty, flooding the alleyways. Seamen carried the girls from a stairwell to the dining hall.

Taking after their mother, the youngsters were not good sailors. The fierce winter storm that dogged their passage across the Atlantic contributed to seasickness. Footlockers banged from one end of the cabins to the other, disturbing sleep at night. They needed to shower clutching a railing.

The dining steward poured water on the white tablecloth to keep plates and glasses from sliding back and forth. And the twelve passengers—five other adults and one small girl—ate with one hand, grasping the table with the other to secure their chairs from charging across the floor. For Sharon's birthday party, the cook made a special effort. True, he produced lopsided brownies and the hot cocoa pitcher pitched over with the waves, but all appreciated his thoughtful efforts.

"The Lord has given us several opportunities for witness on the boat, including a 'church service' on Sunday; although the Lord's Day is not usually observed on this particular boat," Merrel informed Leroy Webber, the Fountain's pastor, "Arlene's Scandinavian descent has helped break down barriers and promote a friendly relationship with captain and crew on this Danish ship."

Thirteen nights later, the *Tekla Torm* entered safe harbor at Casablanca, Morocco.

CHAPTER 20

Constraining Love
1958

C HRIST's love constrained the Callaways (see 2 Corinthians 5:14) to travel thousands of miles across an angry ocean. In Morocco, they hoped to establish a school for missionaries' children.

Map of Morocco, 1960s.
(Map courtesy of Sean Godbold)

A flock of soon-to-become friends met them at the port. Dorothea and Clem Payne and Pete Friesen drove from the town of Khemisset. Don Peterson and Merrel's Hartford cohort Marston Speight sped in from nearer Salé. Marston's excellent French facilitated their quick trip through customs. Even more amazing, they arrived in Khemisset with all their baggage in time for supper that evening! Doris Schneider bounced out of her home to greet the newcomers joyously, along with her quieter husband Bob. After Doris's tasty dinner, the Callaways rode the three kilometers to Sunset Farm, their home for the next four months.

The farm, dotted with citrus and eucalyptus trees and a concrete irrigation tank, housed a yearly conference for Moroccan nationals, boys' and girls' camps, an all-missions conference, and the Gospel Missionary Union conference. In years past it had also hosted a Bible school for national Christians.

The Callaways moved into former cattle stalls. They divided the open area beyond the kitchen/dining room into three bedrooms using furniture and bedsheets. After settling in for a week, they jumped into schooling. Merrel taught the oldest children and Evelyn Stenbock the middle grades. Arlene had the lower elementary classes and Wilma Friesen the kindergarteners.

Each evening after supper, Merrel would slip outside to watch the sky turn shades of brilliant pink, swirling purple-blue, and a blaze of orange-red, validating the name "Sunset Farm."

Pete Friesen cranked up the generator at dusk. Householders hurriedly ironed clothes or did other chores requiring electricity. When the lights flickered briefly, families had ten minutes to light the kerosene lanterns. Stoves and refrigerators ran on gas tanks.

Saturday night baths involved a metal washtub, one kettle of boiling water for bathing, and another kettle to wash and rinse one's hair.

A nearby donkey raucously brayed each morning to awaken everyone. After schooltime, children designed mini-farms in the dry soil, driving their Matchbox vehicles here and there. They took turns sweeping out and up on the long swings hanging between two tall eucalyptus trees. The Payne and Schneider youngsters regaled their new friends with horror stories involving Morocco's successful fight for independence from French rule, secured in 1956.

The Callaway girls guzzled pasteurized milk, until Arlene discovered that the bottles had not first been sterilized. Powdered milk then became the family's fate.

Visits to Khemisset's Tuesday market were always entertaining. Crowds of Berbers (Morocco's indigenous people) streamed in from kilometers around to sell, buy, or barter. Buyers jostled down dusty, crowded rows of merchandise. Sellers displayed enticing towers of seeds and spices—cumin, cinnamon, ginger, aniseed, saffron, sesame seeds, ginger, turmeric, black and cayenne pepper, and paprika.

Assorted bolts of cloth soldiered erectly on counters. Premade clothing hung from hooks, as did raw carcasses smothered in flies. Intricately etched trays and teapots of silver and brass shimmered in the sultry sun. Gravity-defying cornucopias of colorful vegetables competed for customers with the *sphinge*. After these puffy doughnuts turned golden brown in the crackling cauldron of oil, the cook threaded them onto slender reeds, knotting the loop into a handle.

In this mid-twentieth century culture, the barber did double duty as a bloodletter. He inserted two metal tubes into the back of a customer's neck to allow his life force to drip out in a controlled fashion.

The pungent aroma of sheep and goats vied for dominance with that of chickens, mules, and horses.

Riding back to the farm from the market, the family noticed rows of staked grapevines on the left. Merchants shipped their grapes to France for wine. Apparently, US military Commissary shelves housed the only grape jelly in the country. The lines of bright flowers to the right of the road were also sent to France to fashion perfumes.

Arlene and Merrel notified friends back home:

> The month-long Fast of Ramadan is just past. To keep the fast, a faithful Muslim eats nothing from sunup to sundown. How eagerly everyone awaits the nightly signal from the mosque-tower (the minaret), indicating that the sun has set and that they may eat and drink! The nights are full of feasting for the rich, who are awakened at intervals by calls from the mosque. But the poor, who must work in the day and eat at night, find Ramadan a great hardship.
>
> Consequently, tempers are short during this month, which is one of the important tenets of the Muslim religion—one of the Five Pillars of Islam. . . . Not a drop of water is supposed to touch their lips [in the daytime]. Yet, those questioned usually say that despite all they have done, they still have no assurance of salvation.

**Missionary Children's School at Sunset Farm, outside Khemisset, Morocco,
lining up outside chapel**

left to right: Vance, Dean, Sharon, Susan, Julie, Joanna, Joy, Janet, Philip, Linda, Winnona, Johnny, Tim, Grant, Star, Ramond, and Mary, 1959.
(Photo courtesy of Avant)

That summer, the Schneiders brought a black Berber tent back to the States on their furlough to draw attention to the spiritual needs of Berbers across North Africa. The Callaways moved into the Schneiders' house in town across from the Paynes.

**Moroccan Berbers and tent
(Family photo)**

125

Merrel organized the Gospel Missionary Union's conference in June on the farm.

Builders hurriedly erected a house for boarding students. Erma and Don Peterson would be the first house parents there in the fall. An American airbase, Sidi Slimane, donated some "Dallas huts." The military had used these wooden prefab structures during World War II, designed, of course, in Dallas, Texas. Two Mennonite conscientious objector volunteers arrived at Sunset Farm—young "pax" (or peace) men—Gene Kurtz and Roy Landis. They energetically assembled the double Dallas huts. These provided dining and meeting rooms for the large summer conferences and camps. Later, Ben Bubaker joined them in constructing several concrete class rooms. As usual in Morocco, the windows sported bars or shutters or both.

In the whitewashed irrigation tank, Clem Payne baptized Moroccan believers and Joy as onlookers sang "O Happy Day"[1] and "Redeemed, How I Love to Proclaim It"[2] in Arabic or English.

The rest of the summer the Callaways spent in Salé, across the river from Rabat, the capital of Morocco. Merrel and Arlene applied themselves intensely under Marston Speight to beginning Moroccan Arabic—so different from that in the Middle East.

Seventeen students began the new school year. Lois Roth had arrived from French language study in Grenoble, France. She shared the Callaways' home in Khemisset and taught the youngest grades. She provided piano lessons for interested students and played for church and chapel. A devout Moroccan Christian gave the children Arabic language instruction.

Sharon, the oldest student, had a good/bad year. Along with Roy and Gene, she toured several European countries with the Friesens in their camper that fall. As a ninth grader, she took courses through the University of Nebraska High School Extension, so was somewhat free to make her own schedule.

However, a kick from playing soccer reignited the infection in Sharon's leg and ankle. Merrel flew with her to Wiesbaden, Germany, to get medical care at the American army base there.

The Callaway girls relished the curry dinners Arlene prepared. She spread a sheet and pillows on the floor, placing bowls of steaming spicy food in the middle. One night, Miss Roth and the family were seated on

1. Doddridge, "O Happy Day." In the public domain.
2. Crosby, "Redeemed, How I Love to Proclaim It." In the public domain.

the sheet, scooping up the tasty rice and curry with their hands when there was a frantic knock on the door. A bomb had exploded in a coffee house downtown. Could the Callaways come and roll sheets into strips for bandages? They did.

Did the bombing involve a power play between the government and the Berber or *Amazigh/Imazighen* people? Berber is the name the Romans applied to the inhabitants of North Africa, meaning "barbarian." *Amazigh* (singular) and *Imazighen* (plural) was what they called themselves.

About thirteen hundred years previously, Arab Muslims had swept across Morocco and conquered parts of the land. Since then, the Arabs and *Imazighen* had shared the country. In the mid-twentieth century, the government discouraged *Imazighen* political strength and culture and promoted the Arabic language and mores. Was this violence in Khemisset an outburst of these tensions? At any rate, two individuals died in the explosion. Fortunately, someone discovered another bomb in their funeral procession before its detonation.

Merrel and Arlene anticipated the birth of their first child together sometime in the new year. He spoke occasionally at the chapels on American bases, several servicemen finding Christ there. A military nurse-doctor couple came to Sunset Farm, providing free medical check-ups for the children. The doctor expressed concern about Arlene's anemic appearance. Her health was checked out at the military base; all seemed okay. They told her, "If you were having twins, you could deliver here. But since you're not, we can't admit you."

In 1959, Merrel apprised friends, "Arlene stopped teaching on Friday, the doctor ordered her to bed on Saturday, and the babies arrived ten days later. Although they were premature, they are doing well, as is their mother. I am rejoicing in the doctor's unstained record of 'not having lost a father yet.'"

Twins Margaret (Margie) and Martha were heartily welcomed into the Callaway family in February. "A good doctor and a fine hospital have provided excellent care," Merrel wrote, "although not as close to Khemisset as desired. Friends and fellow missionaries have helped in so many ways."

Dorothea Payne and newly returned Ila Davis picked up the teaching slack. (Ila surprised everyone with the latest fashion—the "sack dress.") Elizabeth Speight came for a while to look after the family. Martha and Margie bloomed under everyone's loving care.

School staff treated the student body to a trip to the ancient Roman ruins of Volubilis, about ninety kilometers northeast of Khemisset. A triumphal arch, exquisite mosaic tile floors, and a drainage system revealed a taste of life in an ancient Roman colony. UNESCO has since declared it a World Heritage Site.

Triumphal Arch of Caracalla, Volubilis, Morocco, 2003.
(Photo by author)

Mosaic of the Four Seasons, Volubilis, Morocco, 2003.
(Photo by author)

Basilica, Volubilis, Morocco, 2003.
(Photo by author)

That Easter, Merrel spoke at the Easter sunrise service high on a mountain above Tangier, which fronts both the Atlantic Ocean and the Mediterranean Sea. The Christian Radio station, Voice of Tangier, sponsored the service on their property.

The afternoon before Easter, Voice of Tangier women brought out their massive wooden frame of a cross overlaid with chicken wire. They bordered the cross with lush emerald calla lily leaves, then loaded the wire with masses of creamy calla lilies picked from the hillside. As Merrel preached the precious news of Jesus' resurrection, the flower-spangled cross appeared in triumph behind him.

The Callaways and some others felt that the school should be moved to a city that could provide more activities, schooling choices, and a large English-speaking church for the students. Not everyone agreed. Before the Callaways moved to Morocco, Sunset Farm had provided education just for the few Gospel Missionary Union children in the Khemisset area. Merrel and Arlene had visions of a school for the youngsters of all missions in Morocco. Tangier seemed the logical choice. Besides a good-sized English church with Sunday school teachers, it also contained the American School of Tangier, which the high schoolers might attend. Field discussions were hot and heavy, as some parents did not want their children sent that far north.

After much prayer and debate, the decision was made to move the school to the bustling port city of Tangier. The mission rented property there first. The Mount Washington mansion proved ideal. Arlene wrote, "It is an old 22-room house, large enough to hold the Petersons and boarding children, an apartment for us (total 17 children in the house), an apartment for Lois Roth, school rooms, and other accessory rooms."

In June, Merrel received word that his much-loved Papa had died. Timothy Walton had preached his last two sermons that Sunday at Folly Beach Baptist Church, South Carolina. He had been invited, along with other former pastors, to a Homecoming at Central Baptist Church, Waycross, Georgia. He failed to bring his "Old Dead Mule" medicine with him on the jaunt to Waycross. Friday night, before it was his turn to preach at the reunion the next evening, he suffered a stroke and passed away a few days later. The *Waycross Journal-Herald* reported, "Dr. Callaway loved his native state of Georgia and often said, with a twinkle in his eyes, 'When you go to heaven, you have to go by Georgia.'"[3]

The Petersons, Miss Roth, and the Callaways packed their bags and made the trek to Tangier late in July. Boarding students arrived in the fall. That year, they attended a fast-paced polo match, a horse show, and a symphonic concert. They made bamboo forts and tree forts in the tropical Mount Washington gardens—a perfect place to play capture the flag.

Sharon, a sophomore, and Susan, an eighth grader, were the only students on their level, so they attended the American School of Tangier.

Anna, the Callaways' gentle Spanish maid, looked after the twins while their mother taught the middle grades. At Christmas, as a Protestant, she reproached the Callaways for putting out their nativity scene. She feared that people would think they were worshipping Mary instead of Jesus Christ.

In Khemisset, the family used Arabic in the village shops. During the summer in Salé, they began learning French to use in the stores. Then, in Tangier, buyers needed to know Spanish.

With Spain just across the Straits of Gibraltar from Morocco, Merrel wondered if Spanish Christians could be mobilized to bring God's good news to their Moroccan neighbors. Dr. H. Cornell Goerner, then Area Secretary of Africa, Europe, and the Middle East, Southern Baptist Foreign Mission Board, favored that thought:

> I am interested in your suggestion that the Muslims of Morocco might be reached through Spain. I think there is much to recommend the idea. We are now concentrating on strengthening our

3. Editorial, "A Christian Leader Passes," *Waycross Journal-Herald*, June 23, 1959.

Spanish Baptist Convention and perhaps this might someday be a "foreign mission field" for the Baptists of Spain. If you ever consider a definite mission opportunity for Baptists in that area, I would be very glad for you to bring it to my attention.[4]

The school year went well, though both Erma and Don Peterson suffered poor health. Lois experienced loneliness; Arlene always welcomed her to Sunday dinner. The students discovered two fencing foils hidden in a cupboard of the mansion.

As beautiful as it was with its marble staircase and lush tropical grounds, the Gospel Missionary Union felt it could not afford to purchase Mount Washington. Snippets of an article crafted by Don follow:

> For over a year our Mission has been diligently seeking a permanent location for the Missionary Children's School. . . .
>
> Just on the outskirts of Tangier, three large stone-faced buildings were erected eight years ago. We were informed that the cost of constructing this motel was $54,500 . . . A year and a half ago, the owner was eager to sell the property for $40,000. . . . So, we made an offer of $10,000 and prayed. . . . Last week, praise the Lord, the owners accepted our offer and the first of two payments!
>
> The bottom has dropped out of the real estate market since Tangier lost its international status as a free banking city and as a duty-free port. Many Europeans and Americans have left the country.[5]

After renovation, the staff families moved to their plain but functional new location. Guion Fountain spent a month with the Callaways, who treated him to a whirlwind tour of Morocco. He proudly carried one purchase—his handmade wooden pitchfork—as he boarded the freighter bound for America.

4. Goerner to Merrel Callaway, ca. 1960—1961.
5. Peterson, "Tangier Miracle," in *The Gospel Message*, 2–3.

Callaway family
back row from left: Susan, Arlene, Sharon, Merrel
front row from left: Star, Martha, Margie, Joy, 1961.
(Photo courtesy of Avant)

Reluctantly, the family waved Susan and Sharon off on a plane to the States. They would continue their high school years at a boarding school in North Carolina. Susan did not want to go, but their parents thought their teenage daughters would fare better there.

The School Board voted to name the school Bethel Academy. The balance of the Beth Callaway Memorial School fund went toward the purchase of the land and buildings. Bethel means "house of God" in Hebrew.

The Moroccan government told the USA to remove their bases, so these were closing down. Richard Clinesmith had taught at one of the American bases the previous year. Dick, a sweet-spirited Christian young man, applied to teach at Bethel Academy and was hired.

Lois Roth had her eye on the newest faculty member. In fact, the previous year, she had enjoyed a date with him. But her happiness turned to grief when he then asked out another young missionary woman.

The autumn months, though, showed Arlene and Merrel that the two teachers were definitely interested in each other. Life in a boarding school fishbowl allows little privacy. Merrel and Arlene invited Dick and Lois to join them in an excursion by ferry to the Rock of Gibraltar, to provide privacy for their courting. Once on the Rock, the two couples went their separate ways. Unfortunately, due to the limited landmass, the Callaways and the dating pair kept running into each other! Despite these challenges, the teachers announced their engagement. They wed in a lovely ceremony that February in the British Hope House Church in the Marshan area of Tangier.

Incredibly, the newly purchased property for the school sat right across the road from a riding stable. Col. David, a retired British Cavalry Officer, gave Merrel a good deal on lessons. Two of the older students usually rode Wednesday afternoons. Then on Saturdays, he gave more children a group lesson.

Around November, word came that Sharon's leg had again become infected, but it appeared to heal fairly quickly.

A month later, Merrel and Arlene sent a surprising letter to Mission Headquarters in Kansas City:

> We covet for the Gospel Missionary Union a field in Arabia. Apart from Bethel Academy, I know less about things Moroccan than Arabian and, therefore, feel that we owe it to the GMU to let it be known that we are ready to go to Arabia as soon as possible.
>
> If you look favorably on the idea, we can begin correspondence that would determine whether I would need to make a trip to Arabia first or whether the whole family could move that direction at once. . . .
>
> It must be pointed out that, though many countries of Arabia still seem closed to missions, we cannot be sure of that unless we are knocking on the doors.

Headquarters responded graciously to the Callaways' offer. They felt, however, that they were already overextended in new mission ventures elsewhere. In good conscience, they could not take on another financial burden.

On April 6, 1961, Merrel's Uncle Snap sent Arlene and Merrel an interesting invitation:

> Meck, I feel that the Lord has led you in the work you are now doing. It gave you an important place of service and also helped solve some problems as to the children, their education, etc.
>
> When you and Arlene feel that you would like to return in a closer relation to our Southern Baptist work here or abroad, you would find an open-armed welcome "back home." Our leaders know the circumstances and would be delighted if the Lord should have finished with you in the work you are doing. . . .

> Oceans of love to all your family. My prayers are with you daily.

Possibly part of Timothy Furlow Callaway's reasoning for attempting to woo his nephew back to the Baptist fold was the knowledge that Merrel's heritage included almost forty Baptist preachers. That did not include the many Callaway women who had married Baptist preachers. Timothy Walton, Merrel's father, had written the book *Callaway Baptist Preachers*.[6] His inspiration for crafting the two editions of this work came from a deacon in a Georgia church. This man told T.W. that he had come across numerous Baptist preachers with the last name of Callaway.[7]

Callaway Baptist Preachers
bottom row, left to right: Royall Callaway (Merrel's older brother, who baptized the Plains, Georgia, boy, Jimmy Carter), Timothy Walton Callaway (T.W.—Merrel's father), James Callaway, Timothy Furlow Callaway (Merrel's Uncle "Snap"), and Merrel Price Callaway (Family portrait, inserts by Susan Callaway Anderson)

Uncle Snap planted a seed, which took time to grow.

Gospel Missionary Union missionaries started offering a free Bible correspondence course in Moroccan Arabic. Few signed up at first. But when thousands of advertisements were given out at the Casablanca International Trades Fair, business boomed. Missionaries from several missions began passing out flyers about the course as they passed through towns and villages in their vehicles. Workers struggled to correct the lessons sent in by nearly two thousand seekers. Many more requests followed.

Prayer warriors in America received a new word from Merrel:

6. Timothy Walton Callaway, *Callaway Baptist Preachers 1789—1953*.

7. Timothy Walton Callaway, *Callaway, Baptist Preachers*, Foreword, 1.

The God of all mercy has been good to us and to Bethel Academy. He has provided property at one-fifth its cost to build. He has sent a fine teaching staff and competent house parents. But now that this school for missionaries' children is flourishing in a permanent location, Arlene and I have the opportunity to realize some other hopes of many years. We have longed to get into more direct missionary work than afforded by a children's school, though the latter was an absolute necessity.

In 1958, God led us to begin approaching other missionaries and missions for the increased study of Islamics, as well as Arabic—both Moroccan and Classical. He has abundantly blessed summertime efforts to provide more of the tools needed in introducing Muslims to Christ. Last summer, over 65 missionaries and Christian workers studied together here in Tangier. In the process, Arlene and I have seen how terribly we need Moroccan Arabic, which is so different from the Arabic I have studied.

So, while I am still Chairman of the School Committee, soon I will no longer be responsible for the day-to-day running of the school. This new work will take us to Salé. This means that only the twins will be with us. We will have to leave Joy and Star here in the boarding school at Bethel. Isn't it good that God has raised up a Christian boarding school to care for them?

In her life history written in the mid-sixties, Arlene fleshed out reasons for the move to Salé:

Our first year [in Morocco] was very disconcerting. My husband came with ideas for the school, but ideas prevailing on the field were conflicting and the Field Council exercised complete control of every detail and we were more and more discouraged. It was this fact and, also, that we were not really qualified as elementary school people that led us to request general missionary work, as soon as qualified personnel had appeared on the scene.

Merrel and Arlene applied themselves in earnest to the study of Moroccan Arabic in the spring.

The Petersons furloughed to the States. The mission selected Pete and Wilma Friesen as the new Bethel Academy house parents. Their style was quite different from that of the Petersons.

"In November, 1961," Arlene wrote friends, "we had a letter from Sharon, 17, requesting our permission to be married the next summer after her graduation from high school. We decided that we must go home immediately in order to know how to advise her and be of utmost help." The family drove to Tangier to pick up Joy and Star.

Arlene later disclosed, "Our fifteen-month furlough was a time of great strain and trial."

CHAPTER 21

Fruit Basket Upset

1962

BETHEL Academy students hopped into the gray corrugated van named "the Bethel Star" to wave the Callaways off on the ferry to Gibraltar. In chapel that morning, staff had nixed the hymn, "God Be with You Till We Meet Again,"[1] as "too emotional."

The next day, the family boarded the SS *Christoforo Columbo*, an Italian Line ship, sister to the ill-fated *Andrea Doria*. Hundreds of Italians en route to America were packed like sardines on the tourist-class decks. At least the dreary crossing took only half the time the freighter *Tekla Torm* had taken in the winter of 1958.

And why were the Callaways leaving the field five months early? First, while Merrel and Arlene never unduly pushed their children academically, family tradition held that college followed high school. Regardless of other plans, further education would prepare young people for twentieth-century life and beyond. But Sharon was focused on marriage, not higher education.

Second, Sharon had suffered repeated bouts of severe pain in her leg and ankle over the past fifteen months. Something needed to be done.

Third, Susan was extremely unhappy. Instead of treating her like a normal teenager whose parents were thousands of miles away, the school appeared to assume that the youngsters should all be dedicated foreign missionaries-in-training. Sharon wrote her parents, "My heart goes out to Susan, because she's terribly confused and feels very much alone." Merrel shared, "Arlene and I feel that just now Susan needs the loving firmness and sympathetic understanding of parents, family, relatives, and friends."

1. Rankin, "God Be with You Till We Meet Again," 1880. In the public domain.

The Italian ship pulled out of Gibraltar December 15 and docked at a New York pier December 21. Guion had secured a bungalow for them to rent, picturesquely named Surrey Lodge, just up Long Hill from the Fountains'.

The girls and Arlene sprayed "snow" on the bay window using Christmas-themed stencils. Susan arrived alone from North Carolina on the train, followed by Sharon and her true love from Tennessee. A flurry of Christmas shopping matched the flurry of fluffy flakes falling in New Jersey on Christmas Eve.

The family awoke Christmas morning to find themselves snowbound together after being apart for a year and a half.

But the holidays flew by too quickly. Sharon's fiancé Carl's meat-cutting job at Kroger permitted him only a brief time with Sharon's family. Soon, Susan and Sharon too returned to their boarding school. Star and Joy enrolled in the excellent Chatham Township schools.

Shortly afterward, doctors determined that Sharon urgently required another operation on her ankle. Merrel drove her and Susan northward, where Susan would live with her family and attend the local high school. Doctors Hospital immediately admitted Sharon. Surgery revealed far more infection than they had anticipated. One doctor commented, "The pain to Sharon must have been like that of having three boils all in the same place."

After a month's stay in the hospital, Sharon returned to North Carolina to complete her senior year there. Despite suffering continued postoperative pain, wearing a cast, and maneuvering on crutches, she managed to make up most of her work and graduate in May.

Star and Joy, on arriving from Morocco, had found Gram, their third "mother," drastically different from when they had left her four years before. Parkinson's disease had left her barely able to talk or walk or feed herself. Mrs. Seales, a kindly full-time caregiver, looked after her needs. When Susan and Joy arrived home from school each day, they walked down Long Hill to their grandparent's house for a short visit with Gram. They took turns practicing on their mother's Steinway piano in the parlor.

Sharon's parents made every effort to encourage her to acquire advanced schooling before her marriage. They suggested one good college after another. They also hoped that her young man would complete his degree program first. The military draft possibility loomed over him. But love knows no obstacles. That August, in a beautiful ceremony at Long Hill Chapel, Guion Fountain walked his first granddaughter down the short aisle. Merrel performed the ceremony joining Sharon and Carl in marriage. A simple family reception followed at the Fountain home. Gram sat quietly in her pink rocker, sporting a dainty flowered blouse and a deep-rose velvet skirt.

That fall, Arlene and Merrel agonized over their next step in God's plan for their lives. By this time, Margie and Martha were three, Star was a rising fifth grader, and Susan and Joy were in high school. Merrel wrote a long-standing friend, "We have been going through the most painful time of indecision that I have ever experienced."

Of course, they could continue under the Gospel Missionary Union in Morocco. But other options came to mind.

Merrel had known Paul Freed Sr. when both were missionaries in the Middle East in the forties. His son, also Paul Freed, had begun the Voice of Tangier radio station. The Moroccan government nationalized the station in the late fifties. The founder moved Voice of Tangier to Monte Carlo, Monaco, under the new name Trans World Radio. Between transmitters in Monte Carlo and another in Bonaire above Venezuela, their stations could reach much of the listening world for Christ, including Communist and Muslim nations.

As a younger man, Merrel had had some experience putting on radio programs. He knew the effectiveness of ministry through airwaves. The younger Paul and his dedicated wife, Betty Jane, had spent some time with the Callaways when they lived at Mount Washington in Tangier. Now Paul and Merrel discussed the idea of the Callaways joining Trans World Radio. They could continue to live in Chatham Township as they assisted with programs broadcast into North Africa and the Middle East. This option appealed greatly.

Arlene and Merrel also considered the possibility of joining the Southern Baptist Foreign Mission Board (now the International Mission Board), as Uncle Snap had urged. One of the problems of establishing an indigenous church by a nondenominational mission such as the Gospel Missionary Union was agreement on church government and on second- and third-tier doctrines. The support each family had to raise for these faith missions sometimes had to be spent on either family needs or the needs of the work. There was not always enough money for both.

Dr. B. James Cauthen, Executive Director of the Southern Baptist Foreign Mission Board, expressed eagerness to enlist the Callaways. However, since Merrel had not pastored a Southern Baptist church while married to

Arlene, he would be required to do so for two years before being considered for overseas mission work.

The obvious fourth option was to shepherd a church in the States for those two or more years. Cauthen even suggested that Merrel apply to churches in Virginia and North Carolina. There, they would be closer to Mission Headquarters in Virginia. Merrel sent out letters to preacher friends who might know of churches needing a short-term pastor.

Merrel and Arlene wrestled and prayed mightily to find God's leading. They depended on God at this crucial time regarding finances. Funds were tight. Merrel supplemented their income with speaking engagements. Those barely covered his travel. Their used Packard finally "gave up the ghost" on a trip to see Arlene's mother in Iowa. They returned to Jersey by train.

After many months of uncertainty, the two felt led to return to Morocco under the Gospel Missionary Union for the time being. Receiving the promise of tickets for passage on the SS *Constitution* confirmed their decision. Merrel's friends Marge and Jack Wyrtzen recommended a boarding school in Florida. The school accepted Susan and Joy for the spring semester of 1963. Their father drove them down and said his usual quick goodbyes. Decades later, he confessed, "That was one of the hardest things I've ever done."

Her parents dropped Star off at Bethel Academy in Tangier, then proceeded to Casablanca with Martha and Margaret. The North Africa Mission had opened a language school there. The Gospel Missionary Union Field Council advised the Callaways to continue their Arabic studies in Casablanca. Once the twins got over their "two good cases of chicken pox," they enrolled in Lala Amina's preschool. Several young missionary children lived next door to the Callaways. Margie and Martha named their teddy bears after two of them—Kenny and Johnny.

Merrel and Arlene arranged for Susan and Joy to spend the summer with them. "We have a string of safety pins hanging up in the kitchen," Arlene informed relatives. "Every morning we remove one. When we get to the big one, it will be time for Star to come home, June 14. Then we will remove a few more and it will be time for Joy and Susan to come, June 24."

The three older girls bedded down in the living room. The little ones bunked in their parents' room. A three-day trip to Andalusia in southern Spain highlighted the summer. They toured the magnificent Alhambra in Granada and the Seville Cathedral housing the remains of Queen Isabella,

King Ferdinand, and possibly Christopher Columbus. They chose not to attend a bullfight! Men, women, and children strolled in traditional garb at the vibrant Malaga fiesta. Plaintive strumming of guitars on the warm night air added an evocative Spanish touch.

Summer was soon spent. Students returned to school—Star to Bethel, Joy and Susan to Florida. Merrel and Arlene continued their Arabic studies to better share God's Word with hungry souls. At least, that was the plan.

CHAPTER 22

Regions Beyond
1964

T HE Gospel Missionary Union Field Council surprised the Callaways
with a request. Would they fill in at a bookstore in the bustling city
of Meknes, one of the ancient four capitals of Morocco? Their friends,
Margaret and Maynard Yoder and their children, were leaving for the States
on furlough. They had helped Ila Davis run *Librairie La Bonne Nouvelle*, the
Good News Bookstore, in the business section of the city.

Though still needing more Moroccan Arabic, Merrel and Arlene agreed
to the move. Besides selling secular, educational, and religious books, Ila
and the Callaways taught English, gave Bible classes, and counseled seekers.
Window displays attracted passersby with a clear twenty-four-hour witness
for Christ. "What a thrill it is," exclaimed Arlene, "to place God's Word into
the hands of Muslims for the first time and to tell them the *good news* for
their minds and hearts!"

Margie and Martha attended a French kindergarten, learning more of
that language than their parents. Friendships developed between those two
little girls and single missionary women. Several of them went out of their
way to enrich the sisters' lives. Ila Davis took the time to knit sweaters for
their dolls, which they never forgot.

Margie and Martha Callaway ready for school in their smocks/aprons *(tabliers)*
left to right:
(Family photo)

Star returned to Bethel Academy. Jeanette Jackson, Merrel's niece and sister Mirvin's daughter from James Island, taught the elementary students that year. And Al and Raoma Jessup came as loving house parents.

In May, a smattering of friends and relatives celebrated Susan's high school graduation. Following in the footsteps of aunts and a cousin, she enrolled in Carson-Newman College in Tennessee.

Sharon safely delivered the family's first grandchild—Carolyn Beth.

While ministry at the bookstore continued, Merrel's and Arlene's pioneer spirits saw spiritual needs farther afield. They embarked on a road trip to assess the feasibility of starting work among an unreached people group farther south. Clem Payne, Gospel Missionary Union Field Mission Chair, and his wife, Dorothea, and British missionary Mildred Swan (or "Swannee") and her niece Gay joined them.

Arlene recorded their adventures. Portions follow:

> The first day we drove to Marrakech by way of Kenifra. . . . On Friday, we left in a fog. Most of the way over the high pass in the High Atlas Mountains we could hardly see the road. We were glad when it cleared slightly and let us see where the edges were. Sometimes the road has deep drop-offs on both sides. The Tizi n'Tichka

Pass is over 7,000 feet high. We stopped at a French hotel in Ighre. It turned out to be a very stormy night. We could hardly sleep for the noise of the wind.

The next day, the snow was flying and people were not able to go over the Pass because of strong winds and slippery roads. We were glad to be going in the other direction. We went on to Ouarzazate and had lunch with Kay Richmond, a missionary midwife. We were glad to show Gay the Kasbah where Kay does some of her work. It is one of the old Glaoui Kasbahs, which are all over the South. This man [El Glaoui] was like a tribal chief, who was a leader of chiefs. He chose to cooperate with the French, making it imperative for all the Berber tribes to cooperate. The French would have been in a mess if he had chosen differently.

After leaving Ouarzazate, we found a bridge out on the road. The Simca [French car] had taken this road just fine last trip, but this time we got stuck. It was deeper than we thought because of the heavy rains. It was really funny to see about twenty boys swoop down on our car like a pack of vultures. They watched us drive in. It appeared that they hoped we would get stuck—to add spice to their day and, also, some money. Some of us took off our shoes and waded across, while the boys pushed the car out; and we were on our way.

Then we heard a noise in the car. It was heating up and we found stones in the brakes around the wheels. So, we limped into the next town to have them cleaned out and, incidentally, had a flat tire taken care of in the bargain. After nearly two hours, we were on our way again, with the worst part of the road ahead.

The rain and hail the day before had done lots of damage and several times we wondered if we would make it. We were very glad about 8:30, after dark, to arrive in Tinerhir. We were the only foreigners there that night. The road in the other direction was completely out. The big tourist hotel, which had been completely reserved, was empty.

Monday was market day. We tried to see the *Caid*, the chief governmental officer of the area, about our letter concerning our coming to Tinerhir and my midwifery permit and house, etc., but we weren't able to see him. On Tuesday a.m., we tried once more and were able to see him. He had not even been given my letter, but his secretary produced it. His reply was that there would be no question about my midwifery's acceptance and about my services being wanted here. He said that when his wife had a baby last December, he had delivered her himself. He asked us to wait while his secretary wrote the letter to Rabat for official approval, so I could sign it. He enclosed my midwifery certificate and sent it off. Then he assured us that when the permission came through, he was personally responsible to find us a house and would do so.

Wednesday, we were glad to start on the homeward trail. We . . . arrived back in Meknes about five p.m. Something went wrong with the electrical connection in the car and we were not even able to put it in the garage that evening, but were glad to be home safely.

Merrel announced to friends and supporters:

> Our Mission has taken a new step of faith and outreach. The result is a new push south of the Grand Atlas Mountains, beyond any mission station towards Algeria eastwards and the Sahara Desert southwards.
>
> Arlene Callaway's midwifery is one of the keys the Lord seems to be using to unlock this area for the gospel. Therefore, the Merrel Callaways expect to move south of the Grand Atlas by October.
>
> Thus far, there hasn't been the slightest opposition from any source. But opposition is sure to come, because every advance is bound to be contested.

While Arlene had passed a nine-month midwifery course over a decade before in Assam, she needed to update her skills and knowledge. Merrel agreed she should "spend the month of July at Mother's Hospital in London, doing a short refresher course in midwifery." Susan and Joy came to Morocco that summer. They helped Star look after the household and their little sisters in Meknes. That freed Merrel to continue his work at *La Bonne Nouvelle*.

Arlene found her work in London hard but exhilarating. "The old eight-hour schedule was quite an adjustment after so many years, but I am finding the time here very profitable and am thankful for it."

The southcentral town of Tinerhir sits in an oasis between the Grand (or High) Atlas and the Anti-Atlas Mountains. Only one doctor, a Czecho-slovakian, provided medical care to this town near the Sahara.

"We first applied for a permit to practice in April, 1965," Arlene wrote, "and moved down in October." However, the house they rented required extensive renovations and the unusual rain and landslides made travel difficult. They did not completely move in then.

While on an overseas missions tour, Dr. J. D. Hughey (Southern Baptist Area Secretary for Europe and the Middle East) and Dr. B. J. Cauthen (Executive Director of the Southern Baptist Foreign Mission Board) stopped by Morocco at Merrel's invitation. The Callaways told them about the vast areas of the country still unreached by the gospel of Christ. Merrel drove them up to the northern town of Melilla, still owned by Spain. He showed them the work that Spanish Southern Baptists were doing over the border from Morocco.

Finally, in November, the Callaways settled into life in Tinerhir. The Caid welcomed them gladly, referring to Arlene as "my midwife." The missionaries formed many friendships in the town. Their neighbor, married to an older man, appeared to be in her early teens. She enjoyed playing dolls with Margie and Martha. Electricity in the Callaways' house, which adjoined a restaurant, came on a few hours each evening.

Martha humorously recalls that only her parents and the doctor knew the quality of filet mignon. The other townsfolk just asked the butcher for a slab of beef. Merrel and the doctor tried to beat each other to the vendor to snatch the choice cut.

A visiting British girl, Corinne, "got off the bus with a basket and in it were two live bunnies for the twins," Arlene wrote. They named them "Peter" and "Hoppy." The girls claimed a small shed on their flat rooftop as a hutch. When the pets hopped over to the adjacent restaurant roof, the parents warned that their floppy-eared friends might end up as rabbit stew.

Merrel and Arlene made numerous trips to Rabat to learn the status of her permit application. The dangerous road made travel difficult, especially when flash floods swept through the gorges. Arlene attempted to teach Martha and Margie first grade using a course geared for teachers to use, not parents. And their frequent excursions made it difficult to maintain a reasonable educational schedule.

Arlene wrote, "This has been a rather shattering week." Later, she fleshed out the trouble:

"We finally had word at the end of February, 1966, that I would not be permitted to practice on my Indian certificate. This was a great blow to the Caid, as well as to us. We had come to this new area, where missionaries had never been, and had been welcomed with open arms on the basis of my contribution in midwifery, which is so badly needed."

Merrel described their next step:

> We made a trip to the Provincial Center, Ouarzazate, and went to see the Secretary to the Governor of the Province. On showing him other nursing certificates that Arlene has from the United

States, he was impressed and advised us to send in a second request accompanied by these certificates.

Help is desperately needed for women here. The doctor is a man and all the nurses are men, so women will not come unless they are dying. As someone said the other day, "When they regain consciousness, they flee." We have come to love the people here very much and long to have them come to him who loves them and died for them.

While waiting for word on their renewed request, Merrel and Arlene received news of their first grandson's birth in Georgia—Paul.

Early in May, Arlene and Merrel talked with the Under-Secretary to the Secretary General of the government in Rabat. "It didn't take him long by telephone to look up my file and tell us that the answer was that the permit would not be granted and this would be the final answer. After a great deal of prayer, we decided the only fair thing to do would be to try to become qualified, so we requested furlough."

"Margie's first question yesterday," Arlene said, "when she heard we were going on furlough was, 'Are we coming back? Are we coming back to Tinerhir or going further South?' Martha's first question was, 'How old will Carolyn and Paul be when we see them?'"

But the point of the stateside detour would be for Arlene to earn a US midwifery certificate:

> I am now more or less accepted for a Midwifery Internship Program at the Maternity Center Association in New York City for six months, beginning November, 1966.
>
> Another factor entered into our request for furlough. We are more and more uncomfortable with the extreme separatist position of about half of our supporters and also leaning that direction and away from the Convention of the Southern Baptists of churches that shared our support. We wanted to correct our image in a positive way and our testimony to our friends. So, we have resigned from the Gospel Missionary Union, appreciating all their fellowship, helpfulness, and patience with us, and are hereby applying to the Southern Baptist Foreign Mission Board. We have prayed since our second year in Morocco about the possibility of Spanish Baptists, who are so near North Africa, reaching Moroccans for Christ; and the present interest in Morocco as a field of the Southern Baptist Board, we believe to be the Lord's doing and the answer to our prayers.

Events proceeded quickly after that. The Gospel Missionary Union Field Counsel approved their furlough. Merrel wrote Maynard Yoder, now Acting Chair, an explanatory letter:

> By trying to get another good Board into Morocco, Arlene and I believe we shall be working by multiplication instead of division. . . . We want to leave no stone unturned in keeping and maintaining the same loving, friendly, helpful cooperation in launching out on this, which is simply an expansion of the present fine work being done by the GMU in Morocco.

President Shidler, at the Gospel Missionary Union Headquarters, in his April 12, 1966, letter clearly expressed his disapproval of the Callaways' proposed work under the Southern Baptists in Morocco:

> Due to the extreme political situation, we do not feel that another mission is needed in Morocco. . . . We believe it is not more missions that [are] needed, but more missionaries. . . . We are thankful for your fellowship and membership in the Gospel Missionary Union and, frankly, just do not want you to resign. I would like to ask you to reconsider the matter and we will be praying that God will have his way.
>
> We have all been so very glad that you opened the new station and we do want to back you in any way we can to establish a work there.

Merrel thanked the Gospel Missionary Union Headquarters' staff:

> . . . for the never-failing, thoughtful, and loving welcome we received in Smithfield on our return from Morocco . . . We were greatly touched by your thoughtfulness in offering the position of Southeastern Representatives for the GMU.
>
> We have accepted the offer for the winter of a furnished house in Chatham, New Jersey [the Fountain's home], where Joy will be in college and the three youngest in public school. Arlene has been accepted in her midwifery course . . . We face no alternative than to reconsider our resignation no longer . . . to take effect Nov. 1, 1966.
>
> With confidence that we together can handle this rather delicate business in the customarily beautiful way that has and will glorify him and repeated thankfulness for all you mean to us.

Merrel Price Callaway
(Photo courtesy of Furchgott Studio, formerly in Charleston, South Carolina)

The family flew to New York. They settled into the Fountain home, sharing it with the girls' Great Aunt Rowie. Susan continued at Carson-Newman as a junior. Joy commuted to nearby Drew University and Star began her freshman high school year. Martha and Margie followed their siblings in attending Chatham Township Elementary School.

Arlene updated their friends in North Africa. "My nurse-midwifery internship began November first. Only last year, New York got rid of the last granny midwife. At King's County Hospital in Brooklyn, we work along with medical residents and are accepted. I stay in town most of the week, getting home Saturday and Sunday and usually one night during the week."

Each Sunday morning, Merrel drove the family into New York City. They joined and attended Manhattan Baptist Church. At that time, it had spawned about thirteen daughter churches in surrounding areas. Instead of growing a bigger congregation, they simply planted new churches in various locations.

For Sunday lunch, the Callaways reveled in the tasty and inexpensive ethnic restaurants that dotted the city. They spent afternoons with Gram and Gramp Fountain in Doctors Hospital, where the two lived to provide nursing care for Florence. Before returning to New Jersey, the family dropped Arlene off at her Brooklyn lodging.

God called Florence Prior Fountain home that summer. Her husband said, "Flossie willed her eyes to the Eye Bank, her brain for Parkinson's research, and her clothing was given to Palestinian refugees, which is what she wanted." At his request, Beth's three younger daughters sang, "In the Sweet By and By,"[1] accompanied by their sister Sharon on the piano at their grandmother's funeral.

Meanwhile, Merrel and Arlene reminded their supporters of the Spanish Bible School students that Merrel had lectured to on Islam in Tangier. The possibility of Spanish evangelicals reaching their Muslim neighbors for Christ thrilled the Callaways. They found that Southern Baptists eagerly wished "to advance into this unreached area."

The Southern Baptist Foreign Mission Board accepted the Callaways' application to "serve as missionary associates." A Commissioning Service took place in October, effective December first. "We hope someday to be the first representatives in Morocco." Merrel explained, "It would be some time before we could interest them in Tinerhir, because of the Board Secretary's fear of being misunderstood and accused of taking some other Mission's station."

Once Arlene completed her midwifery course, the two planned to work in Oujda. This strategic center lay in far northeastern Morocco, just a skip and a jump from the Algerian border. Merrel said, "It's a good-sized city, about 150 km. from Spanish Melilla. It's about as far as could be from any existing mission station and still be in Morocco."

The Callaways trusted God for their future.

---

1. Bennett, "In the Sweet By and By." In the public domain.

CHAPTER 23

Thin Ice

1967

O UTREACH in Morocco proved more challenging than usual in the years of 1967 and '68. A misguided religious organization had mailed an un-Christlike tract to the mosques in Morocco. The tract apparently viciously attacked Islam. Instead of exuding the sweet savor of Christ, it increased the desire of Muslims and the Moroccan government to protect their state religion. The government had enough problems with hardline fundamentalist Muslims. They didn't need some supposedly Christian attack making the political climate worse.

Government officials called in numerous missionaries, questioning them about their work. They examined Bethel Academy's legal status, even though no Moroccan students attended that school.

The Callaways arrived into this atmosphere of distrust and uncertainty. They finished up their Berlitz French language course in Casablanca. In Oujda, they found a suitable house with an outbuilding that might serve as a midwifery clinic and located a good used car. Martha and Margie settled into boarding at Bethel in Tangier. The Friesens had returned as house parents.

Star, now a sophomore in high school, enrolled in the American Overseas School of Rome. She boarded at a women's Bible school, the *Instituto Betania* (Bethany Institute). MaryLu Moore, a missionary in Rome with the Foreign Mission Board, agreed to act as her guardian. As she drove Star and her father from the airport, MaryLu asked Merrel what rules Star needed to follow. The teenager held her breath, but Merrel failed to think of any. After the three said their goodbyes, MaryLu basically told Star, "Here's the deal.

If you do well, there will be no rules. If you mess up, we'll rethink matters." Star did well and no rethinking was needed. She loved Rome and enjoyed her school situation.

For Sunday school, sometimes her teacher drove the class around Rome, showing the teens where certain events in the New Testament had taken place. Star liked the girls in the dorm where she stayed, but communication was difficult. Besides English, Star knew a bit of Spanish and more French and Moroccan Arabic. She did not know Italian. The young ladies did not speak English either. However, Conchita, the diminutive housekeeper with a big heart, spoke a little English, so that helped. Star relished exploring Rome. She even received a welcoming letter from the Pope! In her sightseeing, the magnificent Trevi Fountain delighted her most.

Back in North Africa, Arlene and Merrel got to know their new coworkers. Nancy and Joe Newton, with their two young sons, had been living in Spain and knew Spanish. The Newtons felt led by God to start a work in Morocco. They moved to the Spanish town of Melilla, which geographically sat in North Africa. They hoped to branch further afield with ministry to Moroccans. The two couples formed a close friendship. Merrel encouraged them to study colloquial Arabic in Tangier before starting their servant work.

In December, Star tried to confirm the reservation she had made in the fall to fly home for the holidays. The airlines insisted no such record existed. All flights out of Rome that could lead to Morocco were booked! Even efforts by friends failed to wangle a seat for Morocco. The *Instituto Betania* closed for Christmas.

With nowhere else for Star to go, MaryLu Moore graciously invited her to accompany her and her father to Ruschlicon, Switzerland. The car took them through tunnels under the Alps Mountains. MaryLu's sister's family lived in a small apartment at a seminary. They welcomed Star. Unfortunately, there simply was no room for her in their tiny apartment. The fifteen-year-old spent her holiday nights alone in an empty seminary dormitory. She did, however, appreciate the breathtaking views of the Alps each day. In the evenings, she watched locals light bonfires around the lake.

For her younger sisters and parents, the holidays felt subdued without their Star. Christmas morning, they attended the French Protestant Church in Oujda. At the special four o'clock service, they lighted candles on the live Noel tree.

Despite their hopes and dreams of the past years, Arlene and Merrel realized that they should not open a midwifery clinic in Morocco at this time.

In 1968, the Southern Baptist Foreign Mission Board asked the Callaways to work in the Yemen Arab Republic on the Arabian Peninsula for the summer. The newly built Jibla Baptist Hospital desperately needed nurses and support staff.

With hearts overflowing with joy, Arlene and Merrel agreed. Over twenty years before, Merrel and Beth had prayerfully and earnestly tried to bring medical help and the message of Christ's love to the people of Yemen. But that door had remained firmly shut. Now their prayers and a host of others' petitions were answered in the affirmative. The two left in the spring, planning to return to Morocco at the end of the summer.

Passing through Tangier on the way to Yemen, they stopped at Hope House. Years ago, the North Africa Mission had built a hospital, a church, and a residence home for staff and other missionaries there. Dr. Farnum St. John, from England, directed the hospital. Merrel recollects:

> We spent a night or two at Hope House on the Marshan. Since Dr. F. St. John happened to be out of town that weekend, his wife asked me to preach at the Sunday services at the hospital. Before we left Tangier, Dr. Janet St. John said that, since her husband had to be away so often, she wished that we could return to preach in the English service. I gave her no hope for expecting us back.

The Callaways plunged into work in Jibla, a market town in southwestern Yemen. The town spilled over a rugged basalt mountainside of the Baadan Range. Arlene wrote, "The climate in Jibla is nearly perfect, 7,000 feet, cool, sunshine every morning and rain every afternoon (in summer), sweaters in the evening. It's a wild, primitive country in many ways." The two first lived in a cozy duplex high above the hospital, with congenial neighbors next door.

That June, Merrel traveled to Morocco and picked up Margie and Martha from Bethel Academy. Then the three flew to Rome to collect Star. They flew in a DC-3 propeller airplane (from experience named "the Vomit Comet") onto the dirt runway in Taiz, Yemen. As the plane came to a bumpy stop, they viewed wrecked airplanes on one side of the runway and a cemetery on the other. They learned that pilots and crew from the brand-new Yemen Airways were buried there! The terminal consisted of a simple tin hut with a few crude tables and chairs. Martha felt the strangeness of her surroundings; then thought, "Daddy is with me, so everything is okay."

As summer drew to a close, Merrel and Arlene realized that they should continue their current work in Yemen. The political climate in Morocco limited freedom for ministry at that time. Joe Newton wrote them on August 9, 1968, "I was saddened to read of your request for the transfer [from Morocco to Yemen]. Nevertheless, we wholeheartedly agree that your place of maximum service is at the hospital there."

In the fall, Star, Martha, and Margie flew to Good Shepherd School in Addis Ababa, Ethiopia, an excellent boarding and day school run as a collaboration of several mission boards. A survey of Christian boarding schools around the world ranked Good Shepherd School at the top of the list. The younger girls, entering third grade, struggled with homesickness. When classes finished in the afternoons, they headed for Star's dorm room to receive sisterly comfort. After several weeks of this, Star laid down the law. "You may not come to my room again unless you promise not to cry." But for the most part, they had a good time at Good Shepherd.

Merrel kept Mr. Fountain abreast of their situation:

> Arlene and I had a whirlwind visit to Morocco, turning over Tinerhir station to an excellent group and the Oujda station to our former colleagues, Joe and Nancy Newton. The Newtons will "man" it from Melilla, where we have a good church, until a couple can be sent full-time to Oujda.
>
> Star writes, "I love Good Shepherd School!" She was elected Secretary of the Student Council, so they must like her, too!

On their trip, the Callaways said goodbye to some North Africa Mission friends. Due to the recent problems in that country, they deemed it best to remove their headquarters from Morocco to Marseille, France.

For almost thirteen years, Arlene had put her nursing talents on hold. Now she was free to use her extensive training and excellent management skills to bring hope and healing to the hurting in the turbulent Yemen Arab Republic. Merrel would find his own vital place of service there, too.

CHAPTER 24

Arabia Felix
1968

F OR half a century after 1912, the *imams* (religious kings) of Yemen
had locked their country in the Middle Ages. Medicine, finance, transportation, communication, energy, education—all fell woefully behind the
times. The rulers rejected foreigners and foreign ideas. But in the fall of
1962, many Yemeni revolted against the tight-fisted monarchy and fought
to establish a republic. Yemen began to enter the twentieth century.

Map of Yemen
Arab Republic
(YAR) and People's
Democratic
Republic of Yemen
(PDRY), 1970
(Map courtesy of
Steve McCord,
Manager of
Analysis and
Reporting, and
Jim Courson,
Senior GIS
Analyst,
International
Mission Board,
SBC)

The Soviets eagerly shared their expertise with the fledgling nation. The 100 percent Muslim citizens, however, preferred the presence of Christians in their land to Communists. At least Jesus's followers believed in God! Dr. James M. Young, a missionary at the Baptist hospital in Gaza, made exploratory trips to Yemen to ask "if medical missionaries could enter the country."[1] The Yemeni Minister of Health gave Southern Baptists permission to begin medical work there.

Dr. Young, accompanied by his wife, June, began a clinic in the busy town of Taiz. Meanwhile, Young oversaw the building of a hospital in the town of Jibla.[2] Arlene and Merrel helped fill the dire need for personnel there. Their three summer months multiplied into half a decade of intense ministry.

The Swedish Christian builders who had constructed the hospital then began building houses for mission staff. Merrel delighted in the panoramic views out the picture window in their new living room. Six days a week he descended fifty-seven steps to work in the hospital business office. He paid employees, accepted fees from patients with his Yemeni colleague, and collected receipts from the hospital purchasing agent. When Merrel suspected that the receipts had been "doctored," he drove the two hours to Taiz to question merchants. He found that the agent had padded the receipts. The man appeared to use this stolen money to build his family a lovely house.

Math was not Merrel's specialty, though. When he accidentally overpaid some employees, they honorably returned the money to him.

Merrel acquired the roles of director and chaplain of the hospital and treasurer and chair of the mission. He loved to preach! He brought inspiring messages in English to the Swedes, Americans, Palestinians, Egyptians, Spaniards, and Australians who staffed the hospital. He took his turn preaching to the patients in the Sunday night service in the hospital chapel. The men sat in front, of course, as society dictated. The women crowded in the back or in an adjoining room as they listened to the songs and Bible-based preaching. Merrel labored to prepare these messages in Yemeni Arabic, but it was not in vain. Several who had attended these early services later came to faith in Christ.

Of those first years in Yemen, Merrel said, "These two years have been the busiest of my life!"

---

1. Carter, "Yemen—Today and Long Ago," in *Discovery*, 3.
2. Carter, "Yemen," in *Discovery*, 4.

A language teacher came regularly from Taiz to give the new workers lessons in Yemeni Arabic. The Callaways needed to communicate correctly in medicine and in ministry.

Arlene's nursing schedule alternated among the morning, afternoon, and nighttime shifts. For part of her years there, she held the position of Director of Nursing or "Matron." She wrote repeatedly to friends and friends of friends, pleading for qualified nurses for their hospital. To a pal from Assam days, she penned, "I never dreamed that I would be experiencing some of the early problems of another mission hospital!"

And problems there were! Arlene patiently struggled to teach village women how to decipher thermometers. But she pointed out, "When you think that they cannot read or write and have lived behind double black veils for centuries, it's not surprising that they cannot read a thermometer." Before the women could record the temperature correctly on the patients' charts, though, Arlene had to teach them another new skill—how to hold a pencil! She also instilled simple hygiene lessons in the aides.

When Margie and Martha came home on vacation, they loved playing with the little ones in the children's ward. Before they could enjoy that treat, though, their mother made sure they folded towels and sheets and straightened the hospital linen closet—work before pleasure. As they grew older, they took turns helping her with small tasks on night duty.

Workers from other missions and countries staffed the hospital. This sometimes led to misunderstandings and disagreements. The unwanted job of confidant burdened Arlene's shoulders and heart, though she tried to act as peacemaker and counselor.

Besides keeping the home fires burning (Merrel still hadn't learned how to boil an egg), Arlene acted as a gracious hostess for social gatherings among the staff, with Yemeni friends, and among expatriates. Her ability to spread a smorgasbord of culinary delights with little notice was legendary.

Patients flocked from all corners of Yemen and beyond to experience the acceptance, the loving care, and medical expertise at the hospital. Some walked for days over rugged terrain, carrying their children for treatment.

Main entrance to Jibla Baptist Hospital, Yemen Arab Republic, ca. 1971.
(Photo courtesy of the International Mission Board, SBC)

Two Yemeni boys, with town of Jibla in the background, ca. 1971.
(Photo courtesy of the International Mission Board, SBC)

The town of Jibla was remarkably scenic, with its emerald green ter-
races stepping down the surrounding mountains and the narrow houses
perched above of differing colors of stone. But the tall windows open at
the base of each floor proved a fatal hazard for children and adults alike.
And numerous little ones were brought to the hospital with burns from the
smoldering charcoal braziers in their homes. The famous *jambiyas*, curved
daggers belted to men's waists, inflicted grievous wounds.

Medical personnel regularly encountered leprosy, tuberculosis, infantile diarrhea, and bilharzia from worms. Surgeries, the outpatient clinic, complications from childbirth, and inpatient care consumed the dedicated staff's time and energy. The hospital contained sixty to seventy beds. The outpatient clinic often treated over two thousand people each month.

Clinic Day at Jibla Baptist Hospital, Yemen Arab Republic.
Patients waiting outside to get a number, ca. 1971.
(Photo courtesy of the International Mission Board, SBC)

Missionaries hoped that the answer to the constant nursing shortage would be to train their own. They appointed a director of the new Jibla Baptist School of Nursing and recruited eleven young Yemeni men for the class. But first, the students needed to be able to read, understand, and speak English. A six-month English course was begun in late fall of 1969. Merrel recorded the lesson tapes for the students. In spring, the actual nursing courses began. Arlene helped start the school, taught some classes, and trained the student nurses.

An encouraging word came from Kay Richmond in Morocco. She and another woman had developed a thriving ministry to a large group of young girls in Tinerhir. This gladdened the Callaways' hearts. Their attempt to pioneer there was being continued by others.

**Merrel Callaway talking with Yemeni man and boy in Jibla, ca. 1971.
(Photo courtesy of the International Mission Board, SBC)**

A number of staff at Jibla hospital had previously worked in Gaza. This pleased Merrel. He often remarked, "The Baptists learned how to do ministry first in Ajloun and then Gaza." Now, Jibla reaped the benefit of those experiences and knowledge.

The Callaways anticipated a six-month stay in the States beginning in midsummer of 1970. They planned to unwind as they toured several spots in Europe. Arlene wanted to show her husband and daughters her father's country of Denmark. En route, though, they learned that Grand-father Fountain was seriously ill. Merrel and Arlene gave Star the choice of continuing their sightseeing or flying straight to New York. They flew. They spent some time with him at Doctors Hospital, then settled in St. Paul for their furlough. In late September, Guion Hillman Fountain joined his heavenly family.

Come winter, the two youngest girls and Merrel and Arlene returned to Yemen, leaving Star behind to begin a new chapter at Carson-Newman College.

As the hospital in Jibla grew, the need for a liaison between it and government offices in Taiz, Yemen's second largest city, became obvious. The Callaways moved there, renting a home near the post office. Three days a week, Arlene made the long trip to Jibla to continue serving as a nurse. Merrel spent half of his time on hospital business. He taught English and

developed personal relationships with twenty-five young business and pro-
fessional men he had met in government offices.

He began a weekly Bible study and worship time in English in their
home for the many expatriates of varying nationalities. He wrote, "It is the
nearest thing to a regular church service in Taiz and is attended by Arabic-speaking and English-speaking foreigners. Use of the phrase 'regular
church service' is rather thrilling in view of the fact that there have been no
regular services in Yemen for over twelve hundred years!"

Back in Georgia and South Carolina, two Callaway girls each found
"him whom their soul loves." Susan and Brent married in June, Joy and
Blake in October. It was not feasible for their parents or young sisters to
attend.

The People's Democratic Republic of Yemen (PDRY)—also known
as Aden—halted all Christian work in their country. Many feared that the
same would happen in the Yemen Arab Republic (YAR), north of Aden.
The best defense is offense, the Callaways believed. They pleaded with their
mission to open a small midwifery work in the northwestern Yemeni town
of Sa'dah, with its proximity to Saudi Arabia. As much as they loved their
jobs and friends in Taiz and Jibla, Arlene and Merrel requested permission
to move to Sa'dah. They wanted to bring medical care to pregnant mothers,
which could later be expanded to a small clinic. Three factors drove their
thinking: the precarious political situation, the need to "Finish the Task;
Hasten Christ's Coming," and "the undisputed fact that Sa'dah is certainly
one of the 'Uttermost Parts of the Earth.'"

The mission determined that a lack of sufficient staff and money made
the idea unwise. The Governor of the Sa'dah area, however, was most disappointed that medical help would not be coming to his region.

But changes were in the offing.

CHAPTER 25

Torn between Two Loves

1972

S HOCK waves rippled through the Callaways as they read Dr. Hughey's letter of July 5, 1972: "Dr. Cauthen asked whether you would be willing to consider returning to Morocco. You know the country as few others do . . . You are deeply interested in Moroccan people and want [us] to do something for them."

Arlene and Merrel stared at each other. Can this be? Another move? Surely not! Five years ago, they had left Morocco as it was closing down to mission work. Though exhausted, Arlene reveled in her medical work in Yemen. And the day barely held enough hours for Merrel to complete his tasks. They knew the importance of their work, impacting lives for the better. They had grown to love the people of Yemen, just as they loved Moroccans. And now this?

Hughey's letter explained that Nancy and Joe Newton had invested a full term in Morocco, but found it not conducive to the work they wished to do. They had dreamed of opening a school for mentally challenged children. However, they never received a response from their government application. With limited options, Joe had started the Rabat Baptist Fellowship housed in the French Protestant church building. (After Morocco won its independence in 1956, many French settlers returned to France. This shrunk both Catholic and Protestant congregations, emptying many buildings.) Now with young children, though, the Newtons needed to be settled in one place. After their furlough, they would move to a Middle Eastern country with more established work, leaving Morocco without a Baptist witness.

Dr. Hughey ended with this bombshell: "What is your assessment of the situation in Morocco now and the prospects for the future?"

Prayer, debating, more prayer. The Callaways finally agreed to undertake a one-month survey of Morocco with a view to work opportunities for a young couple (or so they thought). French, they knew, would be indispensable as the trade language of Morocco. Merrel and Arlene's French was limited. The Board agreed to provide sufficient funds for this comprehensive survey.

A surprised Dr. James Young and his wife, June, heard about the chance that their coworkers might transfer back to Morocco. In August they wrote, "Most of all we want you to do what you feel God leads you to do." They continued, "Let me just add a word—I can't bear to think of your leaving! We will be anxious to know what your ideas are after a visit there and we will pray with you for the Lord's guidance."

In September 1972, Merrel and Arlene packed in trips to three countries, including seventeen cities and towns in Morocco alone. They discussed the matter with old friends and new friends, interviewing Americans, Britishers, Spaniards, Moroccans, and others. They went to schools, churches, orphanages, and medical facilities. Some reports were discouraging; others invigorating. Some they spoke with saw little future for ministry in the country. Others eagerly welcomed new ideas, new people, new possibilities.

A twelve-page report summed up the Callaways' impressions and findings. They bulleted ten possible projects in numerous towns, cities, and regions in the south, north, west, and east of the land. They concluded that the government would welcome individuals who could make a positive contribution to the welfare of Morocco. Finding a valid *raison d'être* or worthwhile job that would enhance the future of this amazingly beautiful country was the key.

Once again, a decision needed to be made—to go or to stay. Arlene viewed the Lord's will as "90 percent common sense and 10 percent inspiration." Merrel agreed, "The Lord doesn't chew our food for us." They listed the "pros and cons" of moving to Morocco:

Cons:

- Distance from Good Shepherd School in Addis Ababa, for daughters
- Challenging responsibility to start a new venture
- Lack of French language proficiency

- Yemen's abundant need of medical services

Pros:

- Letter from supervisors requesting they consider going
- Rejection by the mission of the Callaways' desire to expand medical work to other needy regions in Yemen, possibly God's way of turning their focus to Morocco
- Supervisors' suggestion that the Callaways know more about Morocco than many others. (Arlene and Merrel's response, "In the kingdom of the blind, the one-eyed is king!")
- The possibility of their making some unique contribution to Morocco

These thoughts spun in the Callaways' minds as they sought God's will. Finally, the existing needs of the Jibla Baptist Hospital swayed the balance. They would stay.

As usual, they welcomed the visit of Dr. Bill Marshall, Field Representative over Cyprus and the Middle East, to their Taiz home. After much congenial discussion and one of Arlene's tasty suppers, Bill prepared to take his leave. As he said his goodbyes, he mentioned that the Board would now shut down its work in Morocco. They did not think it fair or wise to send a young, inexperienced couple there again without seasoned, mature guidance.

As the door closed behind Dr. Marshall, the Callaways looked at each other in consternation. "Now, why didn't he say that much earlier?" True, in his July 5 letter, Hughey had written Merrel and Arlene, "I am turning to you as persons who helped us to accept Morocco as a Southern Baptist mission field." With the knowledge that Morocco would now be closed, the couple reevaluated their decision. Final answer: They would return to the Land of the Setting of the Sun.

The two reluctantly agreed that Merrel should leave for France in January to spend a year immersing himself in French. Arlene would continue her medical work in Jibla until Martha and Margie completed their school year at Good Shepherd School in June. Then she would join her husband in language study.

Pleased with their decision to transfer to Morocco, Hughey nevertheless ruled out the idea of France. "I think we have to face the fact that wherever you study, you will not become fluent in a year. It is probably better to work in Arabic and English and just learn enough French for simple conversations."

The Callaways yielded ground on this issue. Merrel flew to Tangier, rented a small, furnished apartment, and applied for a tourist visa. To their prayer supporters, he wrote, "Please send both Arlene and me a letter saying that you are praying for us and for Yemen and Morocco, two countries whose people we love so much. It is this love for both which makes a difficult move all the more difficult."

CHAPTER 26

Land of the Setting of the Sun

1973

T HE Callaways juggled their two distant lives for five months. Arlene's twice weekly letters flew the 3,600 or so miles to Merrel. She waited anxiously for her husband's less frequent correspondence. Making important decisions without instant communication was difficult.

Merrel sought to establish a ministry that would benefit Morocco. Tourists flocked there for its intriguing culture, superb cuisine, and hospitable inhabitants. But from past experience, the Callaways found that many Americans took a "vacation" from church when traveling or living abroad. The port city of Tangier included French, Spanish, Italian, and British churches and Muslim mosques, but no church for Protestant Americans. Merrel realized that this might be his *raison d'être*—his calling.

He applied to the Tangier authorities for a pastor's permit. The clerk asked, "Where's your church?" Good question! Just then, someone needed the official's attention. Merrel slipped out of the office. He located the French Protestant Church building and talked with those in charge of it. Much of their congregation had returned to France. The Moroccan authorities had threatened to confiscate it if services weren't held there regularly. Merrel asked if he could have services for Americans there every Sunday afternoon at four o'clock. The French were delighted and relieved to rent their building to him for twelve dollars a month.

Merrel eagerly retraced his steps to the permit office. He gave them the address of his new church: French Protestant Building, 34 *Rue Leo Africain, Tanger*. (The street name was later changed to *Rue Hassan Ibn Ouezzane*.)

Meanwhile, back in Yemen, Arlene worked her shifts at the Jibla hospital. Friends had her over for meals; she reciprocated. Still, she missed her husband terribly, penning him countless letters when she should have been sleeping. On the weekends, she returned to Taiz. She continued hosting the Sunday service that Merrel had started in their home. She usually asked friends from Jibla or Taiz or visitors to bring the message.

Once again, the strong personalities of some hospital staff clashed. Once again, Arlene tried to listen nonjudgmentally and to "bear one another's burdens," but it drained her emotionally.

Merrel, too, waxed emotional. He signed his urgent May 2 telegram to Mission Headquarters in the States, "Lonely Heart Callaway."

News came in March. Star announced her engagement to a boy she had met at Good Shepherd School in Addis Ababa. Both attended colleges now in the US. They married in May in Charleston, South Carolina. After their outdoor wedding, they took an extended honeymoon through Europe, Ethiopia, and Morocco. The groom's parents were missionaries in Ethiopia. They asked to host a reception in Addis after Good Shepherd School closed for the summer.

Arlene traveled there to pick up Martha and Margie from school. They enjoyed the couple's second wedding reception. But Arlene was eager to reunite with her own husband. Martha remembers the flight to Morocco. "Mom was like a schoolgirl; she was so giddy at the thought of seeing Daddy!" They debarked expectantly from the plane at Tangier airport.

No Merrel. He had vanished! Even his friends had no clue to his whereabouts. Fortunately, Drs. Janet and Farnum St. John put the weary travelers up for the night. The next morning, they prevailed on the landlord to let them in Merrel's apartment. Obviously, he still lived there. In one corner of the kitchen tottered a five-month tower—a tower of empty corn flakes boxes!

Husband and father walked in the door. Husband and wife threw themselves into each other's arms, hugging and hugging, and then hugging some more. It finally dawned on the girls how much in love their parents really were—how much they meant to each other.

Apparently, Merrel's tourist visa had been about to run out. That meant that he had to leave the county briefly. He decided to pop over to Gibraltar, then return in time to meet their plane. If only the date of their arrival hadn't somehow been mixed up! But now they were together again. They looked forward to the newlyweds' arrival.

Margie and Martha enrolled in the American School of Tangier. Two other teenage girls lived with the Callaways that year and attended the school. Assisted by a Peace Corps nurse, Arlene volunteered at the school. Once or twice a week they checked students' eyes, teeth, and general health, and encouraged parents to remedy areas of need.

As the year continued, the Callaways discovered that the school administration had a poor reputation in the community. Unlike many American schools, the parents had little say in the running of this place. The school board controlled all decisions. They appeared not to care about improving the moral reputation of an organization run in part by American tax dollars.

In October, the Callaways officially constituted the American Church of Tangier. The charter members were Merrel and Arlene. In addition to his preaching and pastoral duties, Merrel was asked by the French and American Consulates to visit sick tourists in the hospital, assisting them in their time of need, and to hold funeral services for American and French individuals. The Callaways advertised the time and place of their American church services in hotels and a local paper, *Le Journal de Tanger*, ran articles in French, English, and Arabic.

To their relief, the Callaways' residence visas were granted.

Dr. Farnum St. John repeated a request his wife had made five years before. Would Merrel help out with the Sunday morning preaching at the Hope House Church next to his mission hospital? St. John left on frequent trips, so they needed someone to fill in then. Merrel agreed, since the American Church met at four p.m.

The Callaways started a Sunday school in their home the following summer. In August, Dr. Farnum approached them with another appeal. Would the Callaways actually move their American Church to the Marshan to the Hope House church building? Merrel thought he saw the benefit of that move. The British Church had been there since the 1800s; it had historic roots. The Callaways agreed. As a precaution, though, they continued to rent the French Protestant church building. They had discovered that four o'clock in the afternoon was a bad time for a church service. It cut into Tangier folks' siesta!

So Sunday morning services met at Hope House. The Callaways began an evening refreshment/church time in their apartment in the evening. Dr. St. John later wrote a touching rephrasing of Esther 4:14, "Who knows whether the Callaways have come to Tangier for such a time as this?"

But what to do about the girls' schooling? Arlene and Merrel weren't about to send Margie and Martha back to American School of Tangier. Despite tactful contacts with the American Consulate regarding it, nothing had improved there. Several other distraught parents searched for a healthy environment for their own children. Though it was thousands of miles away, the Callaways decided to send their daughters back to Good Shepherd in Ethiopia. Good Shepherd School held high standards and the girls had many friends there. On trips to Ethiopia, the parents could swing by Beirut, Lebanon, to liaise with the Arab Baptist Seminary.

As 1975 rolled around, friends Melvin and Cora Smith came to Tangier so the Callaways could take their furlough. Melvin stepped into Merrel's pastoral duties, doing an excellent job. The government, though, took over the British hospital, residency, and church buildings at Hope House. Fortunately, the Callaways had kept up the rent on the French Protestant edifice, so the church resumed meeting there.

The Callaways rented a brick house on James Island, but did extensive speaking around the country. They visited Martha and Margie's grandmother in Iowa. With health fragile, Bessie Olsen lived in a retirement center/nursing home in Harlan, surrounded by family members.

July saw the family back in Tangier. Britishers John and Violet Thompson had opened a bookstore in the city of Fes in 1960, *Librairie de l'Oasis*. They cornered the supply of textbooks for the English section of Fes University. (Daughter Gillian had earlier roomed with a middle Callaway girl at Bethel Academy.) Now, the Thompsons were retiring to England. They wished to sell their bookstore as soon as possible. Merrel received permission from a government Ministry to purchase it. By February, he owned the store in the heart of one of Morocco's most revered cities. Robert McNaughton, a Scotsman teaching at the American Language Center in Fes, helped tremendously in these and future transactions.

After the Newtons left Morocco for the Middle East, Ian Keller and others led the English services at the Rabat Protestant Fellowship that Joseph had begun. Gordon McRostie of the Gospel Missionary Union also stepped into the breach. In fall of 1976, the Fellowship asked Southern Baptists to take responsibility for the work their denomination had started. The American Church of Tangier agreed to sponsor this mission in Rabat, as per government requirements. As Merrel signed the needed documents in Rabat, an official asked for his Tangier church stamp. Pastor Callaway sped the many kilometers to Tangier and retrieved the "silly stamp," relieved to settle the matter. He now added preaching and pastoring in Rabat to his weekly schedule.

With new obligations in Fes and Rabat, besides their work in Tangier, Arlene and Merrel were stretched to the max! How would they, could they, manage?

CHAPTER 27

The Circuit Riders

1977

G OD's Word came through the prophet in Isaiah 40:31: "They that wait upon the Lord shall renew their strength." The Callaways did wait on him as they flew on eagles' wings, or rather, a rickety car, the 800 kilometers each week from Rabat to Tangier, then on to Fes. When they weren't nibbling their meatball sandwiches, they called down heaven on behalf of their work and that of others in Morocco and across the globe. They bathed their extended spiritual and physical families in prayer.

Their usual pattern: Preach at the Rabat Protestant Fellowship on Sunday morning, drive to Tangier for the evening service, head to Fes to mind the bookstore, then return to Rabat about Thursday. Baptisms, funerals, weddings, hospital visits, and counseling were squeezed in, then correspondence, sermon preparation, one-on-one ministry, hostessing, and repeated trips to government offices.

Bookstore front,
Librairie de l'Oasis, Fes,
Morocco, ca. 1981.
(Family photo)

Bessie Olsen had struggled through many disappointments and hardships. Arlene did her best to send her mother what financial support she could through the years. In April, news came that Bessie had passed away at age eighty-seven. Now she was at peace with her Lord.

Besides their own bookkeeping, Arlene took responsibility for the financial books of Gospel Missionary Union while the Gordon McRosties furloughed. These two jobs involved many late nights and close work. One time, the Southern Baptist Foreign Mission Board auditor Richard Kinney and his wife Daisy were due to arrive in the morning to inspect the books. Arlene struggled into the wee hours to resolve a discrepancy. Finally, Merrel slipped out of bed. He offered to finish the task and urged his wife to go to bed. Tired and frustrated, Arlene snapped, "Merrel, you're so heavenly minded that you're no earthly good!" She declined his help. Years down the road, they laughed over that insult or compliment.

Arlene and Merrel became increasingly concerned about the political situation in Ethiopia. Communists had won control of the country, renaming it the People's Democratic Republic of Ethiopia. Democratic it was not! At Good Shepherd School, the students' freedoms were curtailed for their safety. The school enforced the curfews. While Martha and Margie finished their spring term there, by June it was clear that Good Shepherd School as they knew it would not continue.

The girls took their senior year through the University of Nebraska's correspondence program. While the Rabat American School only went through ninth grade, the administration allowed the two to take Advanced French there with the ninth graders. This entitled Merrel and Arlene to be members of the RAS Association, which ran the school. The American Ambassador to Morocco asked the Callaways to be on his task force. The task force recommended that the school expand through the twelfth grade.

In many ways, 1978 proved a hard year. One young short-term couple came to help carry the load. But their judgment in working outside the boundaries of a Muslim church-state made one spouse a liability and they had to be sent home.

A bookstore employee, whom the Callaways had inherited, left for his vacation. They discovered he had stolen cash and tampered with bank deposit slips. He failed to return after his holiday. Two years later, he resurfaced, wanting his job back. It didn't happen.

Arlene and Merrel became empty nesters in July. Margie enrolled in her mother's nursing school in St. Paul and Martha matriculated at West Suburban Hospital's School of Nursing in the Chicago area.

Then Arlene received word that her nephew Jon and her sister Hulda had been in a car accident. Hulda did not survive.

But rainbows do grace the sky. An English-speaking couple came to teach English in Fes in a two-year program and another two came to Rabat. The University of Fes hired Robert McNaughton on their faculty and the University of Rabat added another professor of English. These all assisted in differing ways in God's work. With that extra help, the Callaways could leave Rabat out of their weekly itinerary.

American Baptists formed an organization they named BRIM or Baptist Representatives in Morocco. Aiming to reach "forgotten peoples" or the "unreached people groups," they assisted Moroccan Christians in attending seminaries and in technical career training. BRIM encouraged national believers and supported efforts to work together as an indigenous church.

Merrel's dear friend from Jerusalem days, Finlay Graham, stepped in as Middle East/North Africa representative for the Southern Baptist Foreign Mission Board. Dr. Graham had retired as President of Arab Baptist Seminary in Beirut. He provided great emotional support and wisdom during the next difficult years. The Callaways always relished fellowship with Julia and Finlay whenever possible.

Merrel's nephew Tim Callaway and his wife, Sammi, came to see Uncle Meck and Aunt Arlene. Two years later, the couple helped out in the bookstore for six weeks. The older Callaways had missed three of their children's weddings, two of their high school graduations, three of their college graduations, and the births of several grandchildren. The Board allowed them a quick stateside trip for Margie's college graduation, granddaughter Carolyn's high school graduation, and a peek at their newest grandson, Sean.

God sent Hameed[1] to work with Arlene and Merrel in *Librairie de l'Oasis*. Merrel shared: "Hameed was from a small Berber village. On hearing the gospel over the radio, he accepted Christ and let people know he was a Christian. This resulted in imprisonment in the village jail for two weeks. Hameed then decided that he would be safer in a distant large city, where he could find work now denied him at home."

---

1. Name changed for security reasons.

**Arlene and Merrel Callaway with assistant Hamid at counter of *Librairie de l'Oasis*,
Fes, Morocco, ca. 1981.**
(Family photo)

This young man blessed the Callaways through the years. He was a quick learner, kind, and honest. He required surgery to remove kidney stones. The operation went well, but he continued to have medical complications.

With the rise of Khomeinism and a resurgence of fundamentalist Islam, the political climate shifted in Morocco. Even though the country had signed an international declaration guaranteeing freedom of religion, they interpreted it differently from the intended meaning of the agreement. According to them, you were stuck with whatever belief system in which your parents raised you. That was the total extent of "freedom."

Secret police harassed Hameed, threatening him when he refused to reveal the names of other followers of Christ. They troubled him for any information he might spill about the Callaways. Through all this, Hameed depended on God for strength and discretion.

Two summers after Hameed's surgery, two plainclothes police raided the bookstore when Hameed was there alone. They carried off all the Christian books and Bibles they could identify, along with a large painting of Barbary pirates and a beautiful picture book on Islam. The police sent word a year later that the Callaways could pick up the books, but they were out of the country at the time. Some of the volumes later surfaced around town.

Trouble multiplied. One American coworker appeared before a civil court for his unacceptable public behavior. Fortunately for him, they postponed his criminal court date. Rumors surfaced of severe family problems. Eventually, after agonizing prayer and discussions, his family was encouraged to return home. Merrel and Arlene continued to remember them daily in prayer.

From heartbreak, blessings often flow. In December 1981, President Reagan asked all Americans to leave Libya. Harold Blankenship had pastored an English-speaking church there for many years. "Rock" and his wife, Dorothy or "Dot," regretfully left Libya. After a month in Belgium, they transferred to Morocco. The Blankenships did a superb job co-pastoring the American Church of Tangier. Later, Rock also pastored the Rabat Protestant Fellowship. Its congregation included a cosmopolitan mix of university students and professors, Peace Corp workers, embassy staff, teachers, business personnel, and others.

BRIM sent out a call for more multicultural-minded and multi-lingual persons to pastor English-speaking churches. It took a "leap of faith" by renting French Protestant church buildings in both Fes and Meknes. Two years passed before services began in Meknes. However, Merrel took the challenge of preaching once a month in Fes, while arranging for other speakers the rest of each month. He started regular Wednesday night meetings there, too. Arlene said with a sigh, "Now three people will be needed to replace him when we retire." She added, "We plod on, spread so thin and aching with what never gets done."

The Callaways' status was changed by the Board from "Associates" to "Career" in appreciation of their faithful and devoted service in Morocco.

Margie's status would also change. She and a godly man of obvious Scandinavian descent became engaged. Her parents took ten weeks of furlough due them to see the couple joined in matrimony in St. Paul. A week later, Arlene and Merrel attended Martha's West Suburban Nursing School graduation.

Their bookstore coworker Hameed persuaded a lovely Christian Berber girl, Malika,[2] to marry him (with her mother's approval, of course). Merrel performed the ceremony. As someone lifted the veil off Malika's face, a large visitor in the back of the church belted out, "Wow!" Yes, she was a Moroccan beauty—both inside and out.

---

2. Name changed for security reasons.

The Callaways' youngest, Martha, signed up for a two-year program to explore career options abroad. A young man whose parents were missionaries in Tanzania also applied. The organizers assigned him and Martha to work in the same country. Naturally, the man fell in love with her. After a time, Martha decided she loved him, too. They married in the Chicago area, surrounded by both sets of parents and a great cloud of other witnesses.

In Fes, Muslim Fundamentalists detested that *Librairie de l'Oasis* sold Bibles in many languages, along with other Christian books, textbooks, travel guides, and works on Islam. The Callaways made certain that every book sold had been approved by the government Censor. Fes University courses required the use of the Pentateuch and the entire Bible to gain an understanding of Judaism and Christianity in their history courses. How could students intelligently argue against something if they knew little about it?

Secret police continued to approach Hameed with intimidating questions. A plainclothes officer entered the store one day, saying that they needed him at the police station "for twenty-five or thirty minutes." Those minutes stretched to eighteen days in prison.

Three days later, they hauled in his pregnant wife, Malika. She had already suffered one miscarriage. Arlene obtained a signed letter from a Hindu doctor who advised that Malika risked another miscarriage in prison. He recommended she be allowed to stay at the Callaways', since Arlene was a midwife. They would bring her down to headquarters to answer a few questions, if necessary. The police agreed.

Friends and his wife tried to provide Hameed with food and blankets, but the police insisted they were caring well for him. Right! During this time, the prisoner clung to Psalm 27:14, "Wait on the Lord; be of good courage, and he shall strengthen thine heart. Wait, I say, on the Lord."

In several cities and towns, the authorities interrogated and imprisoned other Moroccans for their faith. Locals knew these believing men and women as "good people." But officials argued that the three-strand cord of "God, King, and Country" made Morocco strong. When any national replaced the belief system of Islam, that supposedly weakened the cord. "Freedom of religion" became hostage to this thinking.

Prayer for these incarcerated believers circled the globe. At ten o'clock one night, Malika and Arlene heard banging on the door. Merrel said:

> When I went down two flights downstairs to the door, there was Hameed. "You have a bathtub. Fill it up with water."

> Forty minutes later, we thought Hameed would never get out of that tub! He had not had a [real bath in prison]. The cement floor on which forty prisoners slept, ate, and did everything else was wetted with a high-pressure hose once each day without ever being dried. That's why Hameed did not hug or kiss any of us until he was sure he was clean with nice warm water.

Authorities released the other Christians at some point. Perhaps those incarcerated for their faith also learned Hameed's lesson. One can worship God better in prison than in a church. He found that you have time "to think and pray and know the Lord's presence."

During his imprisonment, police had closed and sealed shut the bookstore. The Callaways and others made numerous trips to officials to find out why it had been illegally closed. They had scrupulously obeyed regulations, selling only books approved by the censor. The store provided a real service to the University of Fes's English and History Departments.

Merrel contacted US Embassy staff for any information or assistance they might render. They were most sympathetic and helpful. But questions remained: Did this order come from the Minister of the Interior? Was it a problem with local authorities overstepping their bounds? Or did rabid Khomeinism influence this move?

Finally, the Callaways and friends hired a lawyer. They chose a Moroccan who had argued a case for one of the Baha'i faith. Maitre Mustapha,[3] the lawyer, was a staunch Muslim. He held, though, that true freedom of religion would not weaken Morocco but make it a stronger state. The couple paid Mustapha a retainer to take the case, if necessary, to the Moroccan Supreme Court. But the wheels of justice can grind slowly.

Time was running out for the Callaways. Merrel would turn seventy in January of 1986. Retirement loomed. As the stated owner of *Librairie de l'Oasis*, he needed to find a buyer. He certainly hoped to sell it to a like-minded individual. The pastor of one English-speaking congregation seemed a good fit. But then they realized that selling to another preacher would not be a wise move.

The future of the Fes bookstore was put on the Supreme Court docket for December 1985. Often, one can expect a delay or postponement. Miraculously, the case was bumped up to October. The Moroccan Supreme Court overturned an earlier lower ruling which had resulted in the bookstore's remaining closed. Now, the highest court in the land voted in favor of the

---

3. Name changed for security reasons.

bookstore in particular and in favor of religious liberty in general. The court's ruling reaffirmed Morocco's position of religious freedom, showing that the Bible is not a bad book. That was what Maitre Mustapha wanted the world to know.

He made it clear: "I'm a Muslim and believe that Allah can do anything. Since he can do anything, he could make all Moroccans be Muslims; and since he has not done so, who are we to force people or deny them freedom of choice?"

The very day after this momentous decision, a Baptist woman who had shown interest in acquiring the bookstore arrived in Fes. Denise Kelley spent time with the Callaways. They discussed what would be involved in her purchasing and operating the store. Denise's husband, Dr. Fred Kelley, hoped to secure a position as a professor at a university in Morocco.

Meanwhile, interpersonal problems arose within the Christian community. "When we should be united in praying for religious freedom," Arlene bemoaned, "Satan puts a terrible division between believers; so, we are powerless. I feel like a war is raging relentlessly!"

Merrel, like the fictional Clark Kent, was generally a mild-mannered man. He waxed embarrassingly passionate from the pulpit, but, otherwise, he shied away from controversy. Like Superman, however, when he reached his level of tolerance—watch out! The problem or misunderstanding escalated. Merrel "lost his cool—big time!" The following Sunday, he preached "out of a heart of sorrow."

The pain raging in Arlene's face from hyposthenia wore her down. She had suffered from this affliction to some degree since nursing school. The last decade, though, the sharp pains frequently kept her awake at night in agony. She tried to avoid her prescription medication, fearful of the side effects, but the jabs often drove her to take it.

Joyful news arrived in November and December. Two more grandsons enlarged Arlene and Merrel's quiver from Margie and Joy's families.

Though *Librairie de l'Oasis* was not officially open yet, the Callaways met Hameed there and gave him his severance pay—a bittersweet moment. He had been faithful to the end.

Denise Kelley returned to Fes to finalize the bookstore sale in February 1986. According to Moroccan law, Denise had to present a letter from her husband to the authorities, giving his permission for her to purchase the store. In a meeting with Maitre Mustapha, buyer and seller agreed on the price. All systems were go for the sale! The agreement would be signed the following Thursday.

That was a nerve-wracking morning for the seller and the buyer. They were off to Maitre Mustapha's, who held four copies of the contract. They rode in his car to have their signatures witnessed. Stepping down into a grimy basement room, Denise and Merrel met a sloppy young man clutching a messy notebook. They officially signed the documents of sale. Denise muttered, "It's like a thirty-year-old Humphrey Bogart movie!" But the deed was done—praise the Lord!

After church on Sunday, a little over two weeks before Merrel and Arlene's departure from Morocco, someone announced, "Now we will have a roast!" They "roasted" the Callaways, sharing silly, funny, and moving stories about Arlene and Merrel's years there.

Mrs. Kelley arrived again by train on March seventh. The Minister of Commerce had approved the sale of the bookstore. The official papers could be collected in two days. Everyone dearly hoped that the store could be opened immediately, but that would take time.

That evening, Merrel and Arlene stopped to say their goodbyes to Hameed, Malika, and their daughter Aziza.[4] They had tea, talked and prayed and cried. Toddler Aziza couldn't figure out what was happening.

On Thursday, March 10, 1986, the Callaways' plane lifted from Moroccan soil.

---

4. Name changed for security reasons.

CHAPTER 28

Lighting A Candle
1986

RETIREMENT—A curse or a blessing? After years of physical and emotional exhaustion in countries overseas, the Callaways embarked on a whirlwind of ministry in the United States. They spoke to women's and men's groups, to children and to youth groups. They proclaimed the need for Christians to pray, give, and go, so that the uttermost might have a chance to respond to the good news of salvation. Numerous world missions conferences across the South heard Merrel and Arlene's challenge to take Christ to the Muslim world. While Merrel appreciated fried chicken and potato salad, consuming it for lunch fourteen days straight at several conferences grew tedious. Martha suggested they take a breather from retirement.

The retirees relaxed in the Clark Sound cottage Merrel's father had left him on James Island, South Carolina. They added a roomy bedroom with a tiny bath, a garage underneath, and a narrow screened-in porch.

Several of Merrel's relatives lived nearby. When a dying first cousin asked him what "born again" meant, Merrel shared Scripture with him and his equally ill wife. Within a few days they both passed into eternity.

An in-law had suffered from a severe accident, causing brain damage. Arlene and Merrel several times found her lying in the sandy road in various stages of undress. They wrapped her warmly and led her back to her home, but she wandered out again despite all their efforts. Eventually, with help from Merrel's brother, Timothy, they secured a safe place for her in a nursing home.

Priceless time with children, grandchildren, friends, and other relatives scattered across the country enriched their days. They hosted all these in their James Island cottage.

Arlene mourned the deaths of millions of aborted babies in America who never got to enjoy earthly life, liberty, and the pursuit of happiness. With courage in hand, she volunteered at the Low Country Crisis Pregnancy Center. Feeling inadequate, she nevertheless did her best to bring godly and practical counsel to troubled girls and women. The number of couples begging to adopt a child seemed to match the growing abortion rate, which the lucrative abortion industry fueled. Arlene and Merrel climbed one morning on a bus of like-minded activists and joined a peaceful pro-life march at the State Capitol in Columbia, South Carolina. They pressed on despite the rain. Some kind soul handed Arlene an umbrella. She continued to encourage her church friends to support the work of the Low Country Crisis Pregnancy Center with prayer and finances.

At Baptist College of Charleston, Dr. A.J. (Chip) Conyers chaired the Religion and Philosophy Department. Conyers asked Merrel to serve for a year as a Missionary-in-Residence at the school (since renamed Charleston Southern University). Merrel embraced the chance to impart insights learned over a lifetime in international missions. As a resource person, he attended Chip's classes: Comparative Modern Religions and Contemporary Theology: Toward a Theological and Evangelistic Method for Americans. As always, Merrel prepared diligently for these sessions.

After the school year, the college requested that Merrel continue as Missionary-in-Residence another semester. He held usual office hours before classes on Tuesdays and Thursdays. But he and Arlene wished to deepen their contact with mission-minded students. They asked to use a small apartment on campus. During chapel announcements, students were invited to stop by the Callaways' place to chat Tuesday and Thursday evenings. Young people and staff dropped in for refreshments, casual conversation, and inquiries about mission work.

Dr. Conyers wrote, "The feature of the Callaways' approach to students that most impressed me was their sense of the gravity and importance of each student's vocation."[1] He noticed that when someone seemed especially interested in the mission field, "Arlene would pour them another cup of coffee and ask if they could possibly eat another slice of cake."[2]

1. Conyers, "Be on Mission," in *Advanced Bible Study*, 121.
2. Conyers, "Be on Mission," in *Advanced Bible Study*, 121.

At a reception honoring the Callaways at the end of that semester, the Provost said that the Callaways did as much as the school had hoped for from the Missionary-in-Residence program. That night, Arlene recorded, "Thank you, Lord; all glory to You."

One evening, they drove to Baptist College to hear their first contemporary Christian music concert and message. Arlene gave it both a thumbs down and a thumbs up. "Wow! First time for us. Ready to leave after first song. Noisy!!!!! Lights flashing, colors! Oh, my! All songs Christian lyrics. A direct evangelical message. An invitation for salvation. Lord's work—response—wow! Softer music lovely. He got response from audience. Left thoughtful! May have its place, but doesn't appeal to *me*!"

At least two considerations caused Merrel and Arlene to join the historic First Baptist Church of Charleston instead of a closer meeting place on James Island. The couple loved and appreciated excellent music. The musical offerings for those decades overseas, however, were limited. First Baptist's music program enriched the Callaways' retirement years. Another factor guided their choice. Some churchgoers put missionaries on a pedestal and cannot relate comfortably to them. First Baptists, though, accepted them as two more workers in God's vineyard.

As the Callaways' travel schedule permitted, they threw themselves into supporting their church family. For two years, Merrel served as a deacon. The deacon family ministry modeled New Testament servanthood. As such, Merrel served the needs of individuals and families in the church. He took seriously his responsibility as prayer chair of his Sunday school class, combing magazines, bulletins, and relevant newspaper articles to inform and inspire classmates.

Arlene participated in Women on Mission, sharing her perspectives and experience from the field.

The JOY Club, composed of senior adults, sang at retirement and nursing homes and other venues. The Callaways joined in, singing to God's glory.

After years of living God's love before Muslims, the Callaways returned to find their Southern Baptist denomination fractured by strife over second- and third-tier doctrines. They grieved over the animosity and political power play detonated by some across the denomination. The early twentieth-century poet Edwin Markham probably expressed Arlene and Merrel's hearts' desire in his famous verse:

He drew a circle that shut me out—

Heretic, rebel, a thing to flout.
But love and I had the wit to win:
We drew a circle that took him in![3]

One small example of this judgmental approach surfaced at the regular men's prayer breakfast at a local restaurant. Instead of using the time to pray for the needs of a dying world, one gentleman insistently steered the discussion into argumentative channels. He bitterly denounced those who disagreed with his theological position.

The conflict in the denomination was also evident at the annual convention. Several thousand travelers came from across the nation to flock into the stadium. They had arrived to vote for their issues and their officers. But most of them strangely disappeared before the commissioning service the next evening. Only about a thousand took their seats in the huge stadium as candidates pledged their very lives to tell others about Jesus.

Along with the Callaways, many in the denomination mourned that the principles of prayer and proclamation were undermined by a different focus. One daughter asked Merrel, "Daddy, which side of our denomination is right?"

He answered from the heart, "There are godly people on both sides." Yes, Merrel and Arlene preferred to light a candle rather than curse the darkness in other churches.

On a happier note, Merrel and Arlene spent time with one daughter's family overseas, celebrating Thanksgiving and Christmas with two grandsons.[4] Merrel taught workshops to different groups on Islam and on reaching Muslims for Christ. Then they jetted to Singapore to see another daughter and her husband, who worked in business on that diverse island country.

Two years later, the Callaways considered going on a second trip abroad. By then, yet another daughter's family had moved overseas.[5] Merrel hoped to give devotionals and training workshops related to Arab culture and Islam. Grandma Arlene anticipated helping out after the birth of their thirteenth grandchild. They counted down the springtime days to their departure.

Before their trip, they endured the usual inoculations and medical checkups. A doctor called. He reported that Arlene's blood count was low.

3. Markham, "Outwitted," in *The Shoes of Happiness*, 2.

4. Names withheld for security reasons.

5. Names withheld for security reasons.

She explained that hers usually ran low—around 3,000 or so. The doctor countered that hers was 1,000.

"Oh, my!" her diary read. "I said to Meck, 'Maybe another wife has leukemia.'"

CHAPTER 29

On Mission—A New One!

1992

A RLENE'S blood count dropped dangerously low to 0.697, but a painful bone marrow test declared her bone marrow normal. Dr. Christian, the hematologist who had performed the test, saw no reason why the Callaways could not continue with their planned trip. As Arlene's temperature began to rise, though, Dr. Christian asked, "Is there a first-class hospital where you are going?"

There was not.

Wisely, the couple postponed then cancelled their trip. "Your health comes before all else," Merrel told his wife.

Arlene's temperature curiously shot up and down. She spent a total of six weeks hospitalized over the next three months. The medical staff pumped her with antibiotics and blood donated by many friends. Multiple doctors who examined her could not identify the cause of her low white blood and platelet counts. A second bone marrow sample in the fall showed no diseased cells.

During this time, Arlene still endured trigeminal neuralgia in her face. This painfully had reasserted itself in the 1960s and popped up sporadically during the next thirty years. Singing, talking, chewing, yawning, stress, and even sleeping could trigger bouts of unbearable pain. She had consulted numerous doctors through the years, including a prestigious Harley Street specialist in London, England. Nothing permanently helped.

Now, she wondered if her medical issues might be caused by the strong pain medicines she had regretfully taken through the years. But several doctors insisted that those medications were not responsible for her present troubles.

The sharp attacks on her teeth, cheek, tongue, and eye continued. In desperation, she went for a time to an acupuncturist. The wires he carefully inserted in her did greatly lessen the pain temporarily.

When Arlene attended another missions conference, she met a man who had suffered with the same trigeminal neuralgia. An operation at Presbyterian University Hospital in Pittsburg had relieved his pain completely.

Arlene talked the matter over with her husband and doctors. They agreed that the operation might solve her frequent pain attacks. A neurological team in Pittsburg scheduled her surgery for December. Susan flew up from Atlanta to support Arlene and Merrel. A friend of Susan's had arranged transportation for them and food and lodging.

Another blood sample there revealed frighteningly low white blood counts. The doctors believed that Arlene would have a stroke if they operated. Instead, the following day, they excised a bone marrow sample. Before sending her home to South Carolina, the medical staff filled her with six units of blood and a pile of platelets.

Dr. Christian phoned Arlene at 8:15 p.m. on December 18. "The doctors in Pennsylvania think you have leukemia." Yet another bone marrow test confirmed this diagnosis.

Arlene wrote in her diary, "Do I really have leukemia? Perhaps a relief to know something. *It is treatable.* Poor Meck! He's the eternal optimist. So thankful—quite different from Beth in 1953, fifty years ago. No hope then." Beth had had the rare aleukemic leukemia. Arlene's was myelitic leukemia.

Susan and Brent and Joy's family celebrated a bittersweet Christmas with the Callaways. Two days later, Blake drove sons Ty, Sean, Cliff, and Jesse home through an ice storm to Kentucky. Merrel took Arlene and Joy to Roper Hospital in downtown Charleston. Joy decorated the hospital room's bulletin board with the hymn, "Under His Wings."[1] Arlene wrote, "Daddy goes out of the rooms humming that song in the Oncology Ward. Thank you, Lord, for being with us."

A month of chemotherapy began. Arlene again recorded, "Susan came. Daddy took Joy to the bus station. Waiting for blood until 12 a.m. Uptight—can't sleep, can't stop sobbing. Stop it, Arlene! I'm so ashamed of myself—big pity party. Finally realized not looking to you, Lord."

---

1. Cushing, "Under His Wings." In the public domain.

Out of the hospital at the close of January, she purchased turbans at a wig shop. Eventually, she bought a wig that matched her slightly graying brown hair, but found it annoyingly uncomfortable.

Her return home after a month of chemo proved difficult—"uptight, unsettled, couldn't sleep."

In February, bone marrow plugs showed that Arlene was still in remission. But she needed more chemo rounds to consolidate her gains.

Dr. Chip Conyers of Baptist College stopped by her hospital room. Scott Walker, her pastor at First Baptist of Charleston, came later that day. Chip challenged Arlene to accept a new mission from God. She realized, "Meck and I have made our heaven right here—the house ours, making improvements on it, a church we love and are loved, enough money and food we want. But I *did* not want to go out of my way to talk with cancer patients. Now, Lord, I ask you to use me."

"Ask, and it shall be given you" (Matthew 7:7). Dr. Christian approached Arlene with a request. Would she please talk with another leukemia patient who just came in and was fearful? Arlene agreed. God encouraged the patient and his wife through her.

More rounds of chemotherapy.

Leslie, a Christian nurse, asked Arlene to get her Bible and pray with friends and family of a nonresponsive forty-three-year-old dying woman. Mobs of relatives and the lady's pastor filled the room. Arlene ministered to several, then went back to bed. "I kept thinking of her husband in the lounge, so went down there. I had a nice talk with him." The next morning, the husband came in and told her that his wife had died. "I hugged him and promised prayer."

Later, Leslie suggested Arlene see a discouraged Hodgkin's patient. Arlene talked and prayed with the lady and left her a helpful pamphlet on courage in illness.

This time on Arlene's return home, she found peace and rest. God had her on mission and he was in control. Grandson Ty called from Kentucky. "I love you and hope you'll soon be well." Sharon flew in from Texas for a visit.

In May, Merrel and Arlene flew up to St. Paul. Arlene and her Mounds-Midway Nursing School mates celebrated their fiftieth-year reunion.

"Touch and go" described the month of June. On the twenty-second, Dr. Christian told the family that Arlene had a 50 percent chance of surviving the day. Merrel, Susan, Margie, Martha, and two sons-in-love (as she called them) appeared. But Arlene rebounded and left Roper. July saw other immediate family members in and out of the cottage.

Bone marrow tests in September and December showed no evidence of leukemia. Not wanting her to be exposed to germs on a flight to Dallas, Arlene and Merrel cancelled their Christmas trip to Sharon's family. The following day, Arlene told her diary, "Susan called Joy, . . . ordered her not to come if kids sick. . . . Susan could be my daughter—bossy like me—but what a sweetheart!"

Two grandsons were sick, so their family stayed home.

A new report blasted into the new year—"Bone marrow full of leukemia!" Arlene endured another month of chemotherapy. She had named it "shake and bake," for her violent shaking and high fevers.

April notation, "Dr. Christian doesn't know why my bone marrow won't produce . . . permanent damage? Lord, help me trust and not be afraid."

When Beth was dying of leukemia, her father Guion oversaw much of her care. Merrel pastored in Macon, Georgia, during much of her four last months of hospitalization. He made trips to New York City as often as time and meager finances permitted.

Things changed when his second wife became ill. He looked after her nonstop. Day and night, he burned up the roads between James Island and downtown Charleston. As he drove home in the wee hours one morning, an officer ticketed him for exceeding the 35-miles-per-hour school zone speed limit.

Through the months of treatment, Merrel learned to wash and dry clothes correctly, load a dishwasher, and prepare basic meals for himself. He stayed by his wife's side whenever he could.

First Baptist Church members, their new pastor Lamar King, deacon couples, relatives, and many other friends supported Arlene and Merrel as best they could.

The time came. Enough was enough. Together the two prayerfully decided "no more treatments."

As Arlene rested on their bed at home one Sunday afternoon in May, Merrel began to sing. Suddenly, he heard her tiny, thin voice joining in:

> My Jesus, I love Thee, I know Thou art mine;
> For Thee all the follies of sin I resign;
> My gracious Redeemer, my Savior art Thou;
> If ever I loved Thee,

My Jesus, 'tis now.[2]

As they often did, Merrel and Arlene took tea on the porch overlooking the sparkling sound. Joy called, but felt she was intruding on a special, private time between parents.

Arlene logged her last two diary entries in shaky writing:

> May 23, Mon. Psa. 139:23–24 "Search me and know my heart. Try me and search me and know my anxious [thoughts] and see if I know my hurtful way and leaving me in the way everlasting" [Arlene's memory of these verses]. Good night—dark, this a.m.—less cough.
>
> May 24, Tues. Anniversary 1954-1994 40 [years and dates slightly off]. Pardon my iniquity and forgive, for it is gone.

Thursday night, her father called Joy. She asked, "Come?"

"Yes, please come."

Susan beat her there by a day. Roper graciously provided a bedroom in which Merrel could rest from time to time.

Sunday, Arlene Jensen Callaway slipped into a coma. June 2, 1994, Jesus welcomed her home.

Margie and Martha's husbands insisted they fly to the States. Margie and Martha, with Martha's infant daughter, missed being at their mother's bedside by a day.

Shortly after Arlene's passing, Star's husband exclaimed, "I can't believe it! This man just lost his wife and he's going around the cottage whistling!"

But Merrel had not "lost" his partner. He knew exactly where she was!

---

2. Featherstone, "My Jesus, I Love Thee." In the public domain.

CHAPTER 30

Christ the Solid Rock

1994

D R. John Hamrick, pastor emeritus of First Baptist Church of Charleston and founding president of Baptist College of Charleston, gave Merrel a tip. After Hamrick's first wife, Margaret, had died, he would visualize Christ sitting in her usual chair. Merrel took his advice. Arlene had inherited her mother, Bessie's, wooden glider, in which she often sat to read, have devotions, or relax. Merrel found that it did help him grieve Arlene's passing by imagining Christ sitting in her place. He slapped a sign on the bedroom door:

> Arlene is not here.
> The Lord is here with me.
> She is also with him.

Settled on the glider's needlepoint cushion, perhaps Merrel thought back on all that Arlene had meant to him, to their family, and to so many others. Pain, yes; loneliness, yes. But Christ shared his load.

Merrel requested that any donations be sent to the Arlene Callaway Memorial Fund in lieu of flowers. The fund exceeded $4,300. These monies supported work among the 25 percent of the world that knows little of Jesus. The weekly "First Baptist Builder" bulletin of October 7 enthused, "What a marvelous outpouring this represents of love for this great woman. These gifts will impact the kingdom of God for all eternity."

Friends around the world and Merrel's church family rallied around him. After months dealing with the departure of her friend, Susie Redd sent a note to Merrel and his family. Portions of her tribute follow:

Because of Arlene and Christ, many lost people in India, Yemen, and Morocco heard about the Savior . . .

Because of Arlene, many mothers in labor felt her encouragement and her touch of love and concern for them;

Because of Arlene, the newborn babies that she delivered may have learned about Jesus from their mothers, to whom she witnessed;

Because of Arlene and her quiet, unassuming way, I have learned what it means to deny myself, to take up the cross of Christ in redemptive service, and to follow Him.[1]

Sorrow failed to destroy Merrel's sense of humor. He lived Proverbs 17:22: "A merry heart doeth good like a medicine." At a church budget meeting, members discussed the fund for widows and orphans. Merrel raised his hand. "Does it say anything about widowers?" After the laughter subsided, a lady joked that he should get twice as much for being widowed twice.

At his weekly session with a small group, he talked about ways to share Christ with followers of Islam. They discussed ideas for mission. Merrel strongly advocated for missionaries to live among nationals, not be sequestered on mission compounds. To reach people with the gospel, one must reach out to people. Simple.

The big 8-0 for Merrel approached. Pope Urban II, nine hundred years previously, could not have realized how he would influence Merrel's birthday bash. The pope had galvanized what passed for Christendom in Europe by encouraging the populace to march on Jerusalem and the regions around it. He incited them to "take back" from Muslims the lands that Christians considered holy. Of course, these areas had important significance for Jews, Muslims, and Eastern Orthodox Christians. Marchers carried replicas of Emperor Constantine's cross-emblazoned flag as they perpetrated their attacks. Blood of Muslims, Eastern Orthodox Christians, Jews, and crusaders flowed freely, soaking the ground.

Most present-day Americans and Europeans give little thought to the carnage and destruction wrought there. But for many followers of Islam, the massive slaughter on all sides during these Crusades remains a fresh collective memory.

As the nine-hundredth anniversary of these atrocities approached, Christians in Europe and America believed they needed to apologize to the

1. Redd, portion of personal letter to Merrel Callaway and family, October 1994.

descendants of those impacted by the Crusades. They planned "reconciliation walks" through sites in the Middle East.

Age slowed Merrel's agility, but not his passion for Christ's honor. Following Arlene's death, Star and her husband relocated from Singapore to Folly Island, South Carolina, a few miles from Merrel's home. Star coordinated a birthday celebration with her sisters for their father. They reserved the lovely fellowship hall at First Scots Presbyterian Church in the heart of historic Charleston. The morning of the celebration, Merrel prayed: "Lord, I identificationally repent of the Crusades and desire them under the blood of Christ, forgiveness. Help me to apologize and express sorrow to Muslims . . . Have we been holding up your blessings all these centuries of unrepentance?"

The octogenarian did not stop at prayer. After refreshments and short speeches, Merrel delivered a lengthy sermon. He challenged his two hundred plus guests to let Muslims, Eastern Orthodox believers, and Jewish people know that many present-day Christians now repent of the un-Christlike actions done so long ago in his name.

With Arlene no longer present to curb her husband's enthusiasm, Susan tapped on her watch. Time to wind down the message.

Charleston's *Post and Courier* later sent a reporter to interview the birthday man. Merrel spent much of the time explaining "identification repentance" to her.[2] The reporter photographed Merrel arranging books in his postage-stamp-sized study. On February second, Merrel implored God, "Use yesterday's *Post and Courier* article for your glory and for repentance and redemption."

Merrel Callaway among his cherished books in his study, 1996.
(Photo courtesy of *Post and Courier,* Charleston, South Carolina)

2. Shumake, "Retired Missionary," in *Post and Courier,* February 1, 1996.

Goings and comings. Star and her husband returned for two years to the Far East. And First Baptist of Charleston welcomed as pastor Marshall Blalock, who had grown up in that church. A keen friendship developed between Merrel and Marshall.

"Merrel encouraged me personally to become a greater advocate for missions, and, with no small contribution on his part, our church went from having zero members as missionaries to nine serving in various places overseas. He also, along with J.B., gave us a particular heart for . . . North Africa and the Middle East . . . While he retired from service on the field, his heart never retired."[3]

The millennial year saw Star and her husband purchasing a home on James Island. At the same time, Habitat for Humanity hired Star as director of their Dorchester County branch. The new homeowners' marriage faced many challenges. Star did everything possible to preserve their relationship. Finally, she agreed to her husband's demand for a divorce. Her father provided solace and prayer support during those days.

As Star drove him to a memorial service for a friend at Baptist College of Charleston, she asked her father what he would like for his own funeral. He replied briefly, "I just want you to sing, 'On Christ, the Solid Rock, I Stand.'"[4]

Invitations to speak filled some of Merrel's time. After one mission study at his church, a woman there declared his talk "mesmerizing." Star recalls, "He laughed and said, 'She is a very encouraging woman.'"

Time took its toll, though. Requests to speak diminished as Merrel's mental state declined. With infinite tact, Star told her father that he should no longer be driving. He appeared relieved.

When Margie's family returned overseas, Star received new "marching orders." Martha records:

> God made it clear to Star that she was to take care of Dad. She moved in and lived with her father for the next [five] years . . . They developed a deep and lasting friendship. Each weekday morning, as Star headed for work, Merrel would say, "I'll be praying for you." Star credits his prayers for the success she saw in her career as the Director of the Dorchester County Habitat for Humanity.[5]

---

3. Blalock, email message to Star C. Good, July 29, 2020.

4. Mote, "My Hope Is Built on Nothing Less." In the public domain. The first line of the refrain is "On Christ, the solid rock, I stand."

5. Martha Callaway, "Merrel Price Callaway: His Life," 11.

While the JOY Club members loved Merrel, his unusual behavior became a detriment to the group. His cousin Skipper Keith brought him back home after finding him in a confused state down their sandy road. With Star quite a distance away at work every day, she had to hire someone to keep him safe.

Star asked a friend from her Fort Johnson Baptist Church if she would be interested in caring for her father. Cindy Malone had graduated with a degree in social work and a concentration in geriatrics. Unknown to Star, Cindy was between jobs. She accepted the position with delight.

Cindy recalls the mostly good times she and Merrel had together. She loved to hear her charge quote John Greenleaf Whittier's, "The Barefoot Boy,"[6] about the sun-kissed, shoeless lad who enjoyed whistling. And my, how Merrel himself could beautifully whistle! (He could also yodel. "Yodel for us, Daddy," his daughters would implore as the family rode down the highway. And he did.)

Much of the time, Merrel could not focus well. But when he prayed, "he knew exactly what he was saying." More than once, Cindy told his daughters, "The greatest honor of my life was taking care of your dad."

That era, though, came to an end. Protecting Merrel and Star's health and safety required placing him in a memory care center. This occurred after much heart-searching prayer and anguish. As his daughters left him at the establishment, Star, Susan, and Joy confessed the prayer each had prayed the night before: "Please take Daddy home in his sleep tonight."

Two or three weeks later, Merrel fell and broke his hip. Surgery went well. Physical therapy did not. Merrel could not retain the lessons from day to day that the therapist had taught him. Star moved him to a rehabilitation/nursing home facility. He never walked again.

Workers cared well for Merrel. Star stopped by after work. Sometimes she played hymns on the piano in the lounge for the residents. She thanked the staff for the great job they did shaving her father. No, they didn't shave him, they told her. By sleuthing, she identified a Mr. Nepveux as the culprit. Pastor Blalock ratted him out. "Reggie Nepveux was in Merrel's Sunday school class and part of his ministry was shaving older men in the hospital or nursing homes . . . a servant-hearted man in many ways, who thought much of your dad."[7]

---

6. Whittier, "The Barefoot Boy." In the public domain.

7. Blalock, email message to Good, July 29, 2020.

Marshall Blalock summarized Mr. Callaway's life: "Merrel lived with a singular passion, to glorify God that the nations might know Him."[8]

With her father now in his nineties, the thought of going back again overseas pained Margie. In a quiet part of the lounge, she asked, "What do you need, Daddy?"

"To walk with Jesus," he responded. "Jesus will lead us."

She shared her concern about leaving him and two sons in America, not knowing if he understood. But he took Margie's outstretched hand and started singing, "All to Jesus, I surrender, All to him I freely give."[9] Yes, he understood.

Then she showed him pictures of her two youngest. Merrel pronounced the boy "good-looking." The girl? "She's a sweetheart, just like her mother."

That decade replenished Merrel's quiver with three great-grandsons.

One Sunday afternoon, a friend from Star's church anchored his pontoon boat in front of the Callaway cottage. Star suspected he was sweet on her cousin, who lived next door. Wrong answer! Richard Dority invited Star for a spin around Clark Sound. He then wooed her in fine style.

Together, they went to the nursing home. Merrel lay on his bed. Richard announced, "Mr. Callaway, I'm Richard Dority. I've asked your daughter to marry me, but I'd like your permission. I've come to ask for her hand in marriage."

"Well, what did she say?"

"She said, 'Yes.'"

"Well, then, it's all right with me."

In a short service after church one Sunday, the two were wed. There were no attendants. When the time came to exchange rings, what could the bride do with her bouquet? After hesitating, she passed it to the surprised and embarrassed minister.

Two months later, EMTs transported Merrel to Roper-St. Francis Hospital due to double pneumonia. The doctor called Star. She and Richard drove immediately that night to the ER and saw Merrel up to a room. Susan and Brent spent the next three or so days with him.

Blake, Ty, and Joy made a quick trip there on Saturday. Merrel labored hard to breathe and could scarcely make himself understood. Sunday

---

8. Blalock, email message to Good, July 29, 2020.

9. DeVenter, "I Surrender All." In the public domain.

morning, he shocked Joy by belting out the chorus of, "When We All Get to Heaven."[10]

His wise physician transferred him that week to a peaceful hospice center. Cindy Malone wished to minister to Merrel in his last days. She lovingly washed "his feet in preparation for meeting Jesus."

Martha and Margie arrived together. They and Star spent time with their father, though he could no longer talk. Sharon came late Saturday.

Before dawn Sunday morning, January 31, 2010, Merrel Price Callaway passed away. He died in the dark, but arose to the Sonshine.

10. Hewitt, "When We All Get to Heaven." In the public domain.

Epilogue

As Merrel entered the Lord's presence, perhaps Moroccans, Yemenis, Bahrainis, Palestinians, and Lebanese embraced him eagerly. One might imagine them saying, "*Ahlan wa sahlan*, welcome! But now that you and Arlene and Beth are here, who will tell our brothers, our sisters, our children about Jesus?"

Bibliography

Barcus, Alice. "Suffer Little Children." *The Gospel Message*, May 1959, 2–3.

Bennard, George. "The Old Rugged Cross." 1913.

Bennett, Sanford Fillmore. "In the Sweet By and By." 1868.

Bergfalk, Albert J. "Tezpur Hospital Opened on June 18: Joyous Dedication Held Two Months Previous." Photo by Byron Skalman. *The Standard*, June 25, 1954.

Blalock, R. Marshall. Email message to Star C. Good, July 29, 2020.

Blank-Paged Bible, The. The Holy Scriptures of the Old and New Testaments; With Copious References to Parallel and Illustrative Passages: and the Alternate Pages Ruled for MS. Notes. London: Samuel Bagster and Sons, n.d.

Board of Foreign Missions Baptist General Conference of America. *Read and Rejoice! 1954.* Annual Reports from Missionaries in Ethiopia, India, Japan, The Philippines, 1954.

Board of Foreign Missions Baptist General Conference of America. *Read and Rejoice! 1956.* Annual Reports for 1955 of the Foreign Missionaries, 1956.

Board of Foreign Missions Baptist General Conference of America. *Read and Rejoice!* Condensed from the 1953 Annual Reports of Missionaries on Foreign Fields, 1953.

Brown, Lorne E. "This Is Arabia! A Picture-Story by Lorne E. Brown, M.D." *The Commission*, September 1950, 16–17.

Bryans, Robin. *Morocco: Land of the Farthest West.* London: Faber & Faber, 1965.

Callaway, Beth. "Epistles from Today's Apostles: Missionary Mother in Pioneer Field Finds Life Rugged but Satisfying." *The Commission*, May 1948, 1, 22.

———. "From Near and Far." *The Commission*, January 1951, 21.

Callaway, Martha. "Merrel Price Callaway: His Life." Unpublished family memory (July 2016) 11.

Callaway, Merrel and Arlene. "Farewell Letters." *The Gospel Message*, February 1958, 10.

Callaway, Merrel P. "Callaway Recites Thrilling Escape from Strife Zone: Chattanooga Student Describes Experience in Great Britain." *Chattanooga Free Press*, October 21, 1939.

———. "Epistles from Today's Apostles: Baptists of Near East Organize: Missionary Couple Transfers to Arabia." *The Commission*, January 1948, 1.

———. "Schools." *The Gospel Message*, July 1959, 3–4.

———. "We Pioneer for Kingdoms of Arabia." *The Commission*, May 1948, 6–7, 32.

———. "Who Healeth All Thy Diseases." *The Commission*, November 1948, 6–7.

Callaway, Timothy Walton. *Callaway Baptist Preachers 1789–1953.* LaGrange, GA: Fuller E. Callaway Foundation, 1953.

Carter, Frances Tunnell. "Yemen—Today and Long Ago." *Discovery*, August 1973, 2–5.

Cockburn, Andrew. "Yemen United." *National Geographic*, April 2000, 30–53.

Commission, The. "Highways Opened in Arabia." Editorial, March 1948, 18–20.

Commission, The. "Missionary Associates: Employed October and December, 1966." February 1967, 19.

Commission, The, "News: No. 63: Morocco." December 1966, 30.

Commission, The, "News: Staff in Morocco Grows." November 1967, 31.

Commission, The, "Your Mission Fields: Yemen." November 1966, 18.

Conyers, A. J. "Be on Mission." *Advanced Bible Study.* Lifeway. June 30, 1996, 121–22.

Crosby, Fanny. "Redeemed, How I Love to Proclaim It." 1882.

Cushing, William Orcutt. "Under His Wings." 1896.

Danielson, Walfred and Albert Bergfalk, eds. "First Missionary Doctor Sails for North Bank: Five Workers in Group." Photo and article with unnamed photographer. *The Advance Abroad,* October 1949, 1.

DeVenter, Judson W. Van. "I Surrender All." 1896.

Dixon, Tomas. "Jerusalem: Reconciliation Walk Reaches Pinnacle." *Christianity Today,* September 1999.

Doddridge, Philip. "O Happy Day." 1755.

Dorr, Roberta Kells. "Jibla Summer." *The Commission,* April 1970, 12–13.

Dwyer, Kevin. *Morocco Dialogues: Anthropology in Question.* Baltimore: John Hopkins University Press, 1982.

Editorial. "A Christian Leader Passes." *Waycross Journal-Herald,* June 23, 1959.

Featherstone, William R. "My Jesus, I Love Thee." 1862.

First Baptist Builder. "Arlene Callaway Memorial Fund." Charleston, SC: First Baptist Church, October 7, 1994.

Foreign Missions Baptist General Conference of America. *Milestones of the Year: 1954–1955.* Reprint of report of annual meeting Denver, CO, June 22–26, 1955.

Friesen, Pete. "Bethel." *The Gospel Message,* January 1962, 3.

Friesen, Wilma. "The 1958 Building Program at Sunset Farm." *The Gospel Message,* January 1959, 2–3.

Garrison, David. *A Wind in the House of Islam: How God Is Drawing Muslims around the World to Faith in Jesus Christ.* Monument, CO: WIGTake Resources, 2014.

Geniesse, Jane Fletcher. *American Priestess: The Extraordinary Story of Anna Spafford and the American Colony in Jerusalem.* New York: Nan A. Talese, An Imprint of Doubleday, 2008.

Godbold, Joy. "North African Notes." Unpublished article regarding the demise of Christianity through the centuries in North Africa. (Fall 2005).

———. "One Dark Night." *The Commission,* April 1984, 51.

Goerner, H. Cornell. Letter to Merrel Callaway, ca. 1960–61.

Gospel Message, The, "Monthly Periscope: Morocco." November 1960, 12.

Graham, Julia, comp. "Baptist Beginnings in Lebanon 1893–1956, Part I, 'Said Jureidini.'" https:www.scribd.com/doc/175522751/Julia-Graham-Baptist-Beginnings-in-Lebanon-P1–1.

Gruver, Kate Ellen. "A Christian Home for Trans-Jordan." *The Commission,* March 1948, 6–7, 25.

Hagood, Henry J. "Epistles from Today's Apostles: Syria–Palestine." *The Commission,* November 1945, 18.

Harkness, Robert. "Traveling Home." 1938.

Hewitt, E.E. "When We All Get to Heaven." 1898.

Hoffman, Al, Jerry Livingston, and Milton Drake. "Mairzy Doates," Merry Macs, vocalists, 1943. Copyright Sony/ATV Music Publishing Co. LLC, Spirit Music Group.

Hoffman, Bruce. "The Bombing of the King David Hotel, July 1946." *Journal Small Wars and Insurgencies* 31.3 (2020) 594–611. https://www.tandfonline.com/doi/abs/10.108 0/09592318.2020.1726575.

Hurnard, Hannah. *Hinds' Feet on High Places*. UK: Christian Literature Crusade, 1955.

"Isthmian Lines." www.isthmianlines.com/ships.htm#top.

Jenner, Michael. *Yemen Rediscovered*. English edition. London: Longman. Published in association with Yemen Tourism Company, 1983.

Keylor, William R. *A World of Nations: The International Order Since 1945*. 2nd ed. New York: Oxford University Press, 2009.

Kramer, Gudrun. *A History of Palestine: From the Ottoman Conquest to the Founding of the State of Israel*. Translated by Graham Harmon and Gudrun Kramer. Princeton: Princeton University Press, 2008.

Lanier, Sidney. "Song of the Chattahoochee." *Poems of Sidney Lanier, New Edition*. Edited by Mary D. Lanier. New York: Scribner's, 1906.

Lehman, Frederick M. "The Love of God." 1917.

Lindsey, R. L. "Epistles from Today's Apostles: Jerusalem Goes Wild over the News of UN's Decision, Reports Missionary." *The Commission*, March 1938, 1, 22.

Markham, Edwin. "Outwitted." *The Shoes of Happiness and Other Poems: The Third Book of Verse*. Garden City, NY: Doubleday, Page, 1915.

McRae, Jane Carroll. "Hands Wanted." *The Commission*, October 1948, 26.

———. *Photographer in Lebanon: The Story of Said Jureidini*. Nashville: Broadman Press, 1969.

Mote, Edward. "My Hope Is Built on Nothing Less." 1834.

Mullican, Kenneth R., Jr., and Loren C. Tournage. *One Foot in Heaven: The Story of Bob Lindsey of Jerusalem*. Baltimore: Publish America, 2005.

Nickerson, Jane Soames. *A Short History of North Africa: From Pre-Roman Times to the Present: Libya, Tunisia, Algeria, Morocco*. New York: The Devin-Adair Co., 1961.

Orkaby, Asher. *Yemen: What Everyone Needs to Know*. New York: Oxford University Press, 2021.

Payne, Dorothea. "Please Pray for Us!" *The Gospel Message*, April 1962, 2–3.

Peterson, Don. "Tangier Miracle." *The Gospel Message*, July 1960, 2–3.

Presson, George. In telephone conversation with Susan C. Anderson in March 2001.

Rankin, Jeremiah Eames. "God Be with You Till We Meet Again." 1880.

Redd, Susie. Portion of personal letter of condolence to Merrel Callaway and family. October 1994.

Rowden, Rebecca. *Baptists in Israel: The Letters of Paul and Marjorie Rowden, 1952–1957*. Nashville: Fields Publishing, 2010.

Sadler, George W. "Baptist Life: Jerusalem to Belgium." *The Commission*, June 1946, 9–10, 13.

———. "Report from Africa, Europe, and the Near East: Near East." *The Commission*, January 1950, 15.

Scudder III, Lewis R. *The Arabian Mission Story: In Search of Abraham's Other Son*. The Historical Series of the Reformed Church in America, No. 30. Grand Rapids, MI: Eerdmans, 1988.

Shumake, Janice. "Retired Missionary Gets His Due." Article and photo of Merrel Callaway, photo by Janice Shumake. *The Post and Courier* (Charleston, SC), February 1, 1996.

Bibliography

Spafford, Horatio Gates. "It Is Well with My Soul." 1873.

Taylor, Jeffrey. "Among the Berbers: A Journey through Morocco's High Atlas Mountains." *National Geographic*, January 2005, 78–97.

Taylor, Jim. "Morocco." *The Gospel Message*, March 1959, 2–3.

Trexler, Melanie E. *Evangelizing Lebanon: Baptists, Missions, and the Question of Cultures.* Waco, TX: Baylor University Press, 2016.

Whittier, John Greenleaf. "The Barefoot Boy." First published in *The Little Pilgrim,* January 1855.

Wilson, J. Christy, Sr. *Apostle to Islam: A Biography of Samuel M. Zwemer.* Grand Rapids, MI: Baker, 1952. Reprinted 2017.

Yenne, Bill. *Seaplanes and Flying Boats: A Timeless Collection from Aviation's Golden Age.* Illustrated by John Batchelor. New York: BCL, 2003.

Zwemer, S. M. *Arabia: The Cradle of Islam: Studies in the Geography, People and Politics of the Peninsula with an Account of Islam and Mission-Work.* New York: Fleming H. Revell, 1900.

———. "The Glory of the Impossible." *The Commission*, March 1951, 6–7.